CHUMASH

Books by BRUCE W. MILLER

The Caner's Handbook
Handmade Silk Flowers
Chumash, A Picture of Their World

CHUMASH

A PICTURE *of* THEIR WORLD

WRITTEN AND ILLUSTRATED BY

BRUCE W. MILLER

1988
SAND RIVER PRESS
LOS OSOS, CALIFORNIA

Published by Sand River Press
          1319 14th St.
          Los Osos, California 93402

Also distributed by
Phoenix Books
1127A Broad St.
San Luis Obispo, California 93401
805-543-3591

Copies of this book can be obtained by sending $10.95 + $2.00 postage and handling to: Sand River Press, 1319 14th St., Los Osos, Ca. 93402.

Designed by Diana Bistagne
Cover photograph courtesy Musée de l'Homme

10 9 8 7 6 5 4

ISBN 0-944627-51-X

Library of Congress Catalog Card Number 87-62929

Printed in the United States of America

For Susan, John, Robert, William, Jeanne-Marie.

ACKNOWLEDGEMENTS

I WOULD LIKE to thank Janice Timbrook for her comments and corrections, Virginia Crook for trusting me with hard to find books, Sean McKeown for the loan of related material, Bob Alberti, and Sharon Skinner for their kind help with the ins and outs of publishing, Mark Hall-Patton and the San Luis Obispo County Historical Society for permissions and access, Karl Kempton, Mark Hall-Patton, Diana Bistagne, Mary Donnelly, Mike Cowdrey, and Dan Krieger for manuscript corrections, The San Luis Obispo County Archaeological Society for their consideration, Bob Nichols for his quiet encouragement and access to photographs and drawings, Thomas C. Blackburn for permission to quote from *December's Child*, The Smithsonian Institute, National Anthropological Archives for permission to quote the Harrington collection. The Santa Barbara Natural History Museum for permission to quote from their publications. Leon Landon for his informative corrections to the manuscript. Bruce and Patricia Miller for their timely assistance.

I thank the following institutions for permissions to use photographs, The British Museum, Musee de L'Homme, Smithsonian Institution, N.A.A., Ventura County Historical Museum, Mission San Luis Obispo Museum, Santa Barbara Museum of Natural History, American Museum of Natural History, The Catalina Island Museum, Southwest Museum, Museum of the American Indian, Heye Foundation, Museo de America, Museum of New Mexico, and The San Luis Obispo County Historical Museum.

Most of all I would like to thank all the scholars in the field of Chumash studies whose original efforts have made this book possible. John P. Harrington, H.E. Bolton, Fernando Librado, Maria Solares, A.L. Kroeber, Zephyrin Engelhardt, R.F. Heizer, Campbell Grant, Travis Hudson, Thomas C. Blackburn, Janice Timbrook, and Ernest Underhay... to name only a few.

CONTENTS

INTRODUCTION

THE DAY IS hot. Summer dust covers the trail and kicks up under your feet as you pass. At the side of the trail the chia sage has finally lost its bloom. Dry blue flowers litter the ground beneath the bush. An insect zips across the seed laden clusters skirting the taller pale blue blossoms of ceonothus that grows further off the trail.

Ahead, is a large oak spreading darkness across the trail. You look through the faint shimmer of heat coming off the hillside into its gloom. A feathered banner made from crow and seagull feathers hangs deep in the shade of its wide branches. The feathers are endless layers of black on white, and black on white again. You reach out to touch it but you cannot quite move close enough. Around you the air is dead and in the stillness the leaves of the giant oak are black and heavy, the sky has stopped in its phases, yet in front of you, out of reach, the banner twists slowly, round and round.

You look away, turning your face to the sky. Above a large hawk arcs higher in the blue air. Its shadow crosses your face and then rapidly ascends the chaparral covered hillside. The hawk is hunting. You follow its path as it circles and then mounts the sky moving higher in the convection layers until finally it glides off towards the sea. You look back to the feathered banner, but it is gone. It was a dream. A ghost of things past.

*   *   *

Most of what was once Chumash has been lost to us. Today, the artifacts of their civilization have been packed away in museums or obliterated from the surface of the earth by dust and time and housing developments. Concrete and glass buildings and the asphalt impedimenta of modern cities now occupy many of their village sites. And until recently the Chumash people themselves have been scattered to the winds, their prosperous and dynamic culture vanished into the pages of history. Still they deserve our respect and our attention. They lived in the coastal area of Southern California for thousands of years while modern civilization has been here a mere 200. We are the interlopers. At the very least, we owe these truly remarkable peoples a debt of recognition.

The Chumash believed in a great and powerful universe, full of mystery and supernatural forces. For them everything was mutable and in constant flux. Above were the *Sky People*, benevolent if mischievous Gods, and below the *Nunasis*, dark malevolent beings from an inverse world. The Chumash themselves held center stage in *The World of the People*.

Their concerns were manifold, from the demands of daily life, to the continuation and balance of universal forces. Their world was one of good intentions and true integrity.

Here then is my attempt to describe that world. It is meant to be a general guide to an immensely complex subject. I have let my imagination guide me, but not run wild. To generalize is always difficult and there will always be differing opinions. Still I feel the attempt must be made even if it is an imperfect one.

The crux of this problem is inherent in the very definition of the word Chumash. To call the peoples who lived on the central California coast, "Chumash" is a misnomer and yet it is a serviceable label. It is arbitrary at the very least, a name derived from one of their words and foisted on them by Powell in 1891. Yet it has stuck and I choose to use it here. There are other generalizations made, some things labeled "Chumash" are in fact proved in only one area, Ventura, or the Islands and so on. Our knowledge is imperfect and in the face of it I choose to use a wide brush. Those who know the specifics may apply them and disregard the serviceable labels. Such is the scholar's right.

This book has been drawn from many sources, large and small, mostly scholarly, some of which have been long out of print. Hopefully I have done justice to this original research and given credit where it is due. I am profoundly grateful for all those who have come before me, for without them this book would not exist.

HISTORY

BEGINNINGS

MAN IN CALIFORNIA has been dated as far back as the Pleistocene epoch (about 12,000 years ago). It is possible that the State has been occupied for as long as 35,000 years, although some consider this speculation because datable sites and specimens for that time period are so rare.

Solid dating for the Chumash begins around 8000 B. C. with proven continuous habitation of their territory for at least nine thousand years. Whether or not the most ancient of these people were direct forbearers of the historical Chumash is uncertain. What is certain is that they were here, living on the high ground in the shelter of oak trees.

The Chumash were predominantly a coastal people. Their villages were bunched along the shore from Malibu Canyon above Los Angeles extending northward through Estero Bay to San Carpoforo Creek. Along the coast shell heaps mark the sites of the old Chumash villages which are invariably found in close proximity to estuaries and in the canyons and sloughs where creeks wind down to the shore.

The geographical boundaries of Chumash territory circumscribed some 7,000 square miles and relative to most California tribes their territory was vast. They inhabited two hundred miles of the Central California coastline. Santa Barbara, which they called *Syuhtun* is about mid-point on their range. To the east Mount Pinos was a sacred shrine and considered by them to be the center of their Universe. Draw a line between the two and you have found the heart of the Chumash.

They also inhabited the four northern most islands of the Santa Barbara Archipelago, Anacapa (*'anyapakh*), Santa Cruz (*Limuw*), Santa Rosa (*Wi'ma*), and San Miguel (*Tuqan*). Anacapa, with its forbidding shore and parched landscape, is thought to have been occupied only seasonally. These coastal islands are an extension of the Santa Monica mountains and run east to west in a line at a distance of 12-31 miles off the coast. They vary in physical appearance, Anacapa being the smallest and least hospitable and Santa Cruz

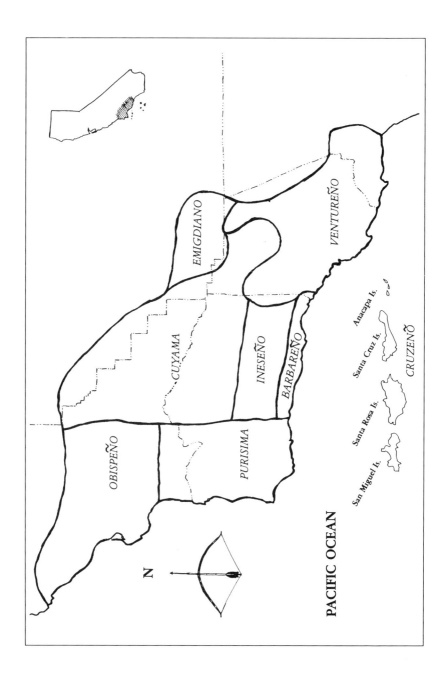

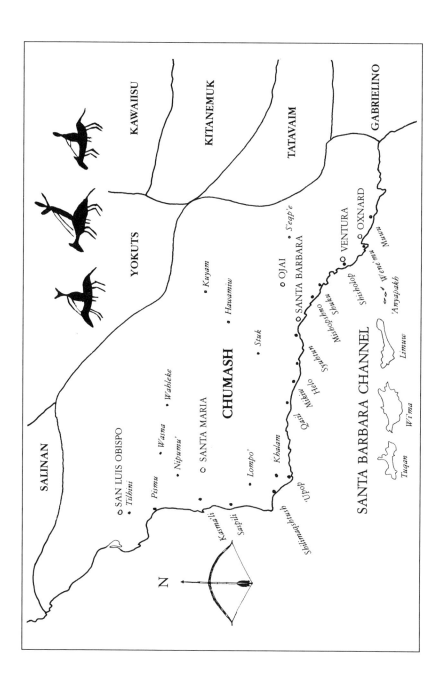

the largest with steep shores. Santa Cruz was called *Michumash* by the coastal mainland people which translates as *"place of the islanders."* Santa Rosa tends to rolling hills and grassland and San Miguel, the furthest out, takes the brunt of the incoming coastal winds such that its dune covered landscape suffers constant erosion.

The Chumash inhabited all of Santa Barbara County, most of Ventura County to the south, and to the north San Luis Obispo County. There is some evidence that permanent Chumash villages extended as far up the coast as Ragged Point on the border of Monterey County line and in the east the Chumash held vast stretches of the Carrizo plain that includes parts of Kern and Los Angeles Counties.

Chumash territory has been divided into eight linguistic regions by A. L. Kroeber, Barbareño, Island, Cuyama, Emigdiano, Santa Ynez, Obispeño, Purísimeño, and Ventureño. Other researchers later used his divisions or very similar ones, such that they are generally accepted today. These names were assigned in the modern era and five of them reflect the missions that were founded in Chumash country (Kroeber 1925).

The natural landscape of the Chumash was rich and varied. From the arid Carrizo plain to the heights of the Sierra Madre mountain range; from the temperate coastal plain to the rugged volcanic shores of the Channel Islands, the Chumash lived and hunted in natural splendor.

Archaeological examination of the living sites of these prehistoric Chumash yield crude flint knives and points, elliptical metates, palm sized manos and rectangular cooking stones. They were a seed and plant gathering people, subsisting on the abundant land resources, the occasional small animal and some shellfish. They built huts into the sides of hills as a sort of earth sheltered subterranean refuge. They buried their dead in the prone position and it is from these burials that we have learned most of what we know of them.

At a later time, the technology of these Indians developed to a level where they made fine projectile points, sandstone bowls, and mortars and pestles. Their refuse sites attest to their skill in hunting. A systematic examination of those sites has yielded the bones of many large animals including deer, elk, grizzly, black bear, and mountain lion. Here were also found the remains of sea mammals, primarily seal as well as large quantities of shellfish. Large fish bones were still relatively rare at these sites (Rogers 1929).

At around 2000 B. C. these prehistoric Chumash reached a high point in bone, shell and stone technology relative to their own past and to other California Indian tribes. They had advanced fishing abilities and the ability to build a swift, multi-planked canoe. They fashioned elegant bone whistles, elaborate incised pendants decorated with shell beads, fishhooks, shell bead money, finely woven baskets and beautiful wooden bowls.

At this time the Channel Islands were continually occupied and an expansive maritime orientation was in full swing. These islands had probably been occupied sporadically in previous millenia (there are radiocarbon dates on Santa Rosa Island from 10,000 years ago) but this may represent a food gathering presence and not a permanent occupation.

These prehistoric Chumash had at their disposal an almost inexhaustible supply of shark, sardines, yellowtail, bonito, and halibut. They developed a trading economy among themselves and with their neighbors. The intratribal trade with the Island Chumash included seeds and the all important acorn, hunting implements — typically bows and arrows, deer hide and rabbit skin, for which the mainlanders received chipped stone tools, digging stick weights, furs, fishhooks, and baskets.

Trade also flourished between nearby groups, the Salinans to the north, the Yokuts to the east and the Gabrielino to the south. It was frequent and beneficial to all so that a Southern California trading economy based on craft specialization developed making the Chumash one of the richest tribes in the area.

They were also culturally rich, with their own music, art, astronomy, and mythology. They began making beautiful rock paintings, whose meaning is in many ways still a mystery today. They developed a strong sense of community and self. They endeavored to control their environment and the very contours of the universe. They had a highly developed sense of ritual and spiritual power which was manifested in their daily life. Above all they had a vibrant, bountiful and relatively peaceful existence.

HISTORY

EXPLORERS

ON TUESDAY MORNING, October 10th, 1542, two small Spanish caravels, *La Victoria*, and *San Salvador* sailed into the Santa Barbara Channel. On board, Juan Rodriguez Cabrillo, commander of the expedition stood tall against the deck railings looking expectantly towards the distant beach. All morning they had fought the wind from the north, tacking back and forth as they followed the shoreline up the coast. Now in the relatively protected channel waters they trimmed the sails and headed closer to shore.

Cabrillo was Portuguese by birth now sailing under the flag of Spain. His chief pilot, Bartolome Ferrelo, motioned to the crew of conscripts and natives to drop anchor and moments later it splashed into the shallow water and sank to the sandy bottom. Above the gold and crimson banner of Imperial Spain unfurled in the stiff coastal breeze as Cabrillo surveyed the scene.

From the shore many Indian canoes flashed across the blue surface of the channel waters, first approaching the Spanish caravels, then circling the gallant flagship swiftly and with apparent ease. Each canoe held twelve to thirteen tanned, muscular Chumash. Most were naked wearing only a waist string, some wore skins or cloaks of sea otter. They were friendly and offered fish to the Spanish (Bolton 1916).

Thus the first contact from the outside world touched the Chumash, signaling the end of one era and the beginning of a new one. A strange new world had come to the Chumash and though little changed by this first visit, the Indians almost certainly took this event as significant, for the Spanish explorers must have seemed truly powerful to them.

The purpose of Cabrillo's voyage, which had started at Navidad, Mexico, on the 27th of June, was to explore the coast of New Spain and look for a new route to China. Three months later he had sailed far enough north to discover *Alta California* and a small land-locked port which he named San Miguel, later to be called San Diego. He was greeted by Indians at San Diego, Santa Catalina Island, and by the Chumash on entering the Santa Barbara Channel.

Cabrillo first landed near a Chumash village along the coast of what is present day Ventura. On landing he took formal possession for the Crown of Spain and named the populous Chumash village *Las Canoas* in respect to the many canoes possessed by the Indians.

On the 14th of October, continuing up the coast, Cabrillo and his crew made landfall again near Carpinteria. All along the way they saw villages and more natives in canoes. The Chumash boarded the caravels and pointed out the *rancherias* (the name the Spanish gave to Chumash villages). There were many including *Shuku, Mishopshno, Shalawa, Syuhtun, 'Alkash,* and *Qasil.* *The Diary Of The Voyage* commented on this part of Cabrillo's journey:

> "All these towns are between the first *rancheria, Las Canoas,* which they call *Xucu,* and this point (five miles west of Point Goleta). They are in a very good country with fine plains, and many groves and savannahs. The Indians go dressed in skins…and they wore their hair very long and tied up with long strings interwoven in the hair; to the strings they attached gewgaws of flint, bone and wood…They say that in the interior there are many - *rancherias*" (Engelhardt 1923:5,6).

That day sailing north, they passed the three largest of the Channel Islands, which Cabrillo mistook for one large island. For the next few days the Indians went with the ships and Cabrillo handed out presents. In return the Indians gave the Spanish "many fresh and very good sardines" (Bolton 1916).

Cabrillo continued up the Channel with good winds until he reached Cape Galera (Point Concepción). Here trouble started, when storms and rough water compelled them to take refuge at wind swept San Miguel Island for a week. Further tragedy struck when Cabrillo fell and broke his arm near the shoulder, an injury which later caused his death.

The storm let up slightly, but Cabrillo was in great pain and the crew was miserable from rough weather. They were driven about off the mainland until finally making anchor at the *rancheria, Las Sardinas* (Gaviota Pass), where food, water and wood were at hand thanks to the friendly Chumash.

In all, Cabrillo anchored seven times in the Santa Barbara Channel; at *Las Canoas,* Rincon, Carpinteria, Point Goleta, *Canada del Refugio,* Gaviota Pass, and Point Concepción.

In spite of the pain of his broken bone Cabrillo and his intrepid crew set sail north. On the way they met another storm and the two caravels were separated. The *San Salvador* and the *Victoria* continued on separately and the *San Salvador* listed its farthest point north as 38 degrees and 31 minutes (Fort Ross), on November 11. Four days later, heading south, they sighted the consort *Victoria* and Cabrillo's crew rejoiced. On the southern leg of the journey they named the Sierra Nevadas, and *Bahia de los Pinos* (Drake's Bay).

Rounding Point Concepción they again harbored at San Miguel Island and there passed the winter. On January 3, 1543, Juan Rodriguez Cabrillo, explorer, and captain of the flagship San Salvador, died from his injury.

Bartolome Ferrelo, a native of Levant and chief navigator, was designated as captain by the failing Cabrillo who charged him not to leave off exploring. Ferrelo voyaged north but met with storms again, so he quickly returned, taking refuge in what is now called Smugglers Cove at Santa Cruz Island. Ferrelo commented:

> "The Indians of these islands are very poor. They are fishermen and eat nothing except fish. They live in houses that can hold fifty people and go about naked" (Engelhardt 1923:11).

Meanwhile the bad weather separated the caravels again and the *Victoria* struck some shoals on San Miguel Island. The crew, thinking they were lost, stripped down to their skivvies and made promise to the Blessed Virgin that if saved they would make a pilgrimage to the nearest church.

The *San Salvador* sailed south to *Las Canoas*, and waited. They later sailed to San Diego and waited again. When finally the *Victoria* appeared there was much celebrating and the two Spanish caravels set sail south arriving at their starting point, La Navidad, on Saturday, April 14th, 1543, where the sailors of the *Victoria* made good their vow.

The next significant visitor to the Chumash was Sebastian Vizcáino who sixty years later on May 5th, 1602, set sail from Acapulco with three ships, *San Diego*, *Santo Tomás*, and *Tres Reyes*. His mission was to survey and explore the California coast and to make maps of possible ports.

Northward along the coast they went, stopping first at San Miguel Bay, so named by Cabrillo which the devoted Vizcáino now named San Diego after the saint of that day and his flagship. On December 4, 1602, Vizcáino passed San Buenaventura and entered the Channel, which was named for the St. Barbara's feast day (Bolton 1916).

With Vizcáino were three Carmelite Fathers, Fr. Andres de la Asumpcion, Fr. Antonio de la Ascencion, and Fr. Tomás de Aquino. Father Ascension left a journal of the voyage. He wrote:

> "After we left San Diego we discovered many islands in a line one after another. Most of them are inhabited by many friendly Indians who have trade with those of the mainland. From the mainland a petty chief came with his son and eight oarsman to visit us, saying that he would entertain us and provide us with anything which we needed and he possessed. The petty chief see-

ing that there were no women on board then offered by signs to give everyone ten women apiece if they would all go to his land, which shows how thickly populated it is" (Bolton 1925:118).

Vizcáino had intended to stay in the Santa Barbara Channel at the invitation of one of the Indian chiefs at San Buenaventura but within an hour after the Indian departed a southeast wind arose. So they set sail and that night and most of the next day the wind was at their back and the navigation was very pleasant.

It wasn't until April of 1603 that Vizcáino returned from the north, probably to pass though the Santa Barbara Channel again. There is no written account except to say that they finally reached Acapulco on March 22, 1603.

It is surprising that for the next 166 years the Chumash were left in peace and no other outside visitor touched their shores. Perhaps other navigators visited the Channel but there is no record of them doing so. Thus these several visits were the last for more than a century and a half. What the Indians thought of this is not known (Grant 1965).

On Monday, August 14th, 1769, Don Gaspar de Portolá heading a party of sixty-five (some accounts list 63 men) on the first land expedition to New California, arrived at the head of the Santa Barbara Channel. They camped in the vicinity of a Chumash village near the site of what later became Mission San Buenaventura. This village they named *Asuncion de Nuestra Senora*.

Portolá was a bachelor at midlife and in his prime. A career officer in the army, he had once fought in Italy and Portugal before finding service in New Spain.

Thus Portolá became the man who was given the task of establishing Spain's claim on the territory of *Neuva California*. This was to be done first by exploring and secondly by establishing permanent settlements much in the fashion that had been used in Mexico over the past two hundred years.

Portolá first went by horseback to San Diego. From there he went northward with a pack train of one hundred and eighty animals and his sixty-five men, a column that stretched out for a full kilometer behind him. Scouts were in front, then Commander Portolá, followed by Ensign Miguel Costansó, and in turn Lieutenant Pedro Fages, and a half dozen soldiers dressed in six ply deerskin vests, each carrying a sword and musket and lance. Then perhaps came two Franciscan friars on mules, Juan Crespí and Francisco Gómez. Behind them was a hundred animal pack train with a dozen mounted drivers alongside and bringing up the rear were the rest of the animals and a company of soldiers (Squibb 1984).

Crespí, Fages and Costansó all kept journals and it is from those records that we get a glimpse of the Chumash in their natural state (Grant 1965).

Portolá broke camp and left *Asuncion* the next day, traveled two leagues and camped near another *rancheria* which the soldiers named for the Chumash Chief who was an excellent dancer. They called it *El Pueblo del Ballarin*. Fr. Crespí commented that "the Indians were quite kind but that they played weird flutes all night and kept us awake."

The village consisted of about sixty tule thatched houses in the shape of half oranges. There were also seven canoes which were used for fishing in the Channel.

On Thursday, August 17th, they set out early and followed a westerly course that lead to the sea. Here they came upon another village which was situated on a beach which forms a kind of bay. On this slight peninsula there were thirty eight huts. Crespí related that not far away the soldiers and scouts found another large *rancheria* near some springs of pitch (Bolton 1927).

> "The Indians here have many canoes and they were just finishing a new one so the soldiers named the *rancheria Carpinteria*, while I called it *San Roque*" (Engelhardt 1923:21).

At *Carpinteria* they received more gifts of broiled and fresh fish. The next day they were accompanied by the Indians, traversing the plain in a westerly direction until they came to the ruins of a *rancheria*. The Chumash that accompanied them said that Indians of the Sierra had come down three months ago and killed all the inhabitants. Five miles further on they came on another village which had suffered the same disastrous fate. It was also at this time that they started noticing an abundance of bear tracks.

For the rest of the week they traveled northwest up and down the potreros and across plains of the mainland coast. All along the Channel they found villages.

Portolá's expedition had a good supply of trade beads and ribbons which they exchanged for baskets, feather work and animal skins. To eat they were given dried fish, acorns and other cooked foods. On Sunday they camped between two *rancherias*.

> "Towards evening the chiefs of each village came one after the other, all in their finery of paints and feather ornaments, holding in their hands split reeds, the motion and noise of which served them to keep time for their chants and dancing" (Engelhardt 1923:25).

Crespí went on to note that in this *rancheria* and in others through which they traveled near the Channel the Chumash had cemeteries.

> "On each grave was a high pole painted in different colors. From the poles that surmounted the graves of men hangs their hair which is undoubtedly cut from the corpse before it is buried, while from the pole on the graves of women swing wicker baskets."

Crespí noted the presence of a large number of whale bones and a basin hewn out of stone that he speculated could have been used for holy water or baptismal font. This was probably a steatite bowl used by the Chumash for cooking and or ceremonial purposes (Bolton 1927).

From this point the caravan moved overland to Oso Flaco and then into Price Canyon in the succeeding days. On Wednesday, September 6th they made camp in a valley that the soldiers called Los Osos because of the many bears roaming the countryside. Crespí gives us a vivid account of that day's sport.

> "The soldiers went out to hunt and succeeded in killing one with bullets, in doing which they learned the ferocity of these animals. When they feel themselves wounded they attack the hunter at full speed and he can only escape by the dexterity of his horse. They do not yield until they are shot in the head or the heart. This one that they killed received nine balls before he fell which did not happen until one struck him in the head. Some of the soldiers were fearless enough to chase one of these animals mounted on poor beasts. They fired seven or eight shots, and I have no doubt he would die from the balls; but the bear upset two of the mules and it was only by good fortune that the two mounted on them escaped with their lives" (Squibb 1984:25).

The Portolá expedition left Los Osos and crossed the Santa Lucia mountain range, leaving Chumash territory. To the north, Portolá was unable to recognize Monterey Bay from Vizcáino's brief description but he traveled far enough to discover San Francisco Bay. Portolá returned along this same route in the winter of 1770 somewhat dispirited after missing his supply ship at Monterey and on January 24, 1770, they arrived back at the little outpost of San Diego. All in all it was a relatively trouble-free trek of some twelve hundred miles. This historic journey marked the beginning of the end for the

Chumash. And the man who would change their lives more than anyone before or since this time was waiting at San Diego. His name was Father Junipero Serra.

Later that same year, in the spring, Portolá set out from San Diego on another trek north through Chumash territory, again looking for Monterey Bay and this time he found it in May of that year. A month later Father Serra sailed north to Monterey to establish the second mission after San Diego. He called it *San Carlos de Monterey*. It was only a few short years before he would start mapping out the fate of the Chumash (Grant 1965).

THE MISSION ERA

FATHER JUNIPERO SERRA was born in Majorca in 1713. His name Serra is a Catalonian form of the Castilian word *sierra*. He taught for a number of years at the University of Majorca before going to Mexico in 1749. In Mexico City, he was assigned to the Apostolic College of San Fernando along with two of his former students, Juan Crespí and Francisco Palou. Later, in 1767, he went with Portolá to Baja California and presided over some of the missions there.

Serra was a man of slight stature, no more than five foot three inches and very thin but at fifty-four years of age, he was an able administrator and a man of unwavering conviction in his mission to convert the California Indians. Possessed of an indestructible optimism, true stubborness and extreme devotion almost to the point of religious fanaticism he was determined to create a utopian California (Bean 1973).

Altogether the Franciscan fathers founded five missions in Chumash territory: San Luis Obispo, 1772, San Buenaventura, 1782, Santa Barbara, 1786, La Purísima Concepción, 1787 and Santa Inés, 1808.

The Franciscan priests of course had the Indians' interests at heart. Theirs was a utopian vision. It was their intention that the Indians would be drawn into the mission system, baptized, taught trades, and then released to be productive citizens. It was thought that this would take approximately a decade after which the Indians would be given farmland and lead the lives of good Christians. Good intentions however are not always manifested in history.

San Luis Obispo (1772) was the first mission to be founded within Chumash territory, and was the fifth mission in the chain of 21 missions that would eventually stretch the as far north as San Francisco Bay. Soldiers came south from the foundering mission in Monterey where food was scarce and starvation threatened. They made their way across the Central Coast hunting bears where they had found them plentiful three years earlier when Portolá had passed that way.

Father Serra, also on his way south from Monterey met them at The Valley of the Bears (Los Osos) on August 19, 1772. He camped there several weeks making preparations and then on September 1, 1772 he raised a wooden cross, suspended a bell from a sycamore tree overhanging San Luis Creek and then dedicated the new mission, *San Luis Obispo de Tolosa*. Soon after, he headed south to San Diego to meet two supply ships. He left a few soldiers and Father Joseph Cavaller behind to tend the new mission. Father Cavaller's flock consisted of a scant two neophytes.

The supplies at the new mission were scarce, and consisted of fifty pounds of flour, three bushels of wheat and a box of brown sugar to be used as barter with the Indians (Angel 1883).

The mission was situated on a gentle hill with a stream at its base. The water flowed year round and was enough for immediate use as drinking water and as irrigation for the crops that were soon planted. By the end of that first year there were four families of Indians converted and living at the mission. There had been no Indian village in the immediate vicinity of the mission but a *rancheria* was soon founded and a relationship was established. The Indians brought venison and seeds, thanking the soldiers for killing many of the bears in the area. Thus the the mission was maintained and began to thrive.

Pedro Fages, who was lieutenant with the Portolá expedition remarked on the Chumash at San Luis Obispo.

> "The hair is worn flowing and is of fine texture. The women wear toupes made by burning and their coiffure is of shells. On their cloaks or skirts, stained a handsome red, they put as a trimming or decoration various fabrications made from tips of shells and small snail shells, leaving numerous pendants hanging from the margin, after the style of the trinkets of our children...The men wear the hair tightly bound and gathered at the back, forming a short heavy queue, with a very handsome adornment of shells; they also wear collars and bracelets of snail shells and little sea shells. The few men who desire to cut their beards accomplish it not without great pain, by using a pair of shells of the clam or large oyster, which being fastened together on one side by nature, can be given a kind of opening and shutting motion on the other. With these they extract the hairs one at a time by the root as though pulling with nippers" (Priestley 1937:31-53).

In the year 1775 a large band of hostile Indians from the San Joaquin Valley set fire to the thatched roof of the mission with burning arrows. The surprise attack came at night and the neophytes valiantly roused themselves to fight. The attacking Indians were driven off but not before the mission buildings were engulfed in flames. In all the mission was burned three times, including once during Christmas Mass. Several of the fires were of mysterious origin and the Padres, fearing such events would be repeated, rebuilt the mission with a tile roof. The Mission San Luis Obispo is credited with starting this trend of tile roofs which was later adopted at all the California missions. The Mission San Antonio in some reports is also credited with this innovation.

Travel through Chumash territory was still infrequent but around this time in 1774, Captain Juan Bautista de Anza set out on the first of two overland expeditions to upper California. The purpose of the first expedition was to find a good land route from Sonora to Monterey, which he did, and the second was to bring with him settlers, sheep and cattle in support of the mission system.

The first Anza expedition of 34 men left Tubac, a presidio south of present day Tucson, Arizona, in January 1774. They moved north and crossed the Colorado with the aid of the Yuma Indians. They headed immediately into the harsh Colorado desert and became mired and lost for six days in large sand dunes. Struggling back to the Colorado River, their animals dying at a rapid rate, the expedition recuperated while the animals were set to pasture. Setting out once again they headed west along what is now the Mexican border passing through the Anza Desert and Borrego Valley and then over the mountains through Royal Pass. By March 22, they had reached Mission San Gabriel which had been founded a scant three years earlier and which now provided safe refuge, although little food, as they were in the midst of their own famine.

The Anza expedition continued north, through Shoshonean territory and on up the coast where the Chumash met them as they traversed the coastal plain near Santa Barbara. Moving further north they stopped at the new Mission San Luis Obispo and then went on to Monterey. Along the way Anza was generous with trade beads and smoking tobacco, spreading them liberally among the Indians. He also made careful maps, noting the fertility of the soil and availability of fresh water (Grant 1965), (Bolton 1930).

The second Anza expedition began in 1775 and is primarily important for its founding of the presidio and mission at San Francisco. The settlement of San Francisco was an attempt by the Spanish to stop the southerly advance of the Russians.

This second expedition consisted of a small group of soldiers attached to Anza. There were also thirty soldiers with families and four civilian families, who intended to remain in California as *pobladores*, or settlers. Altogether with the Fathers Font, Garces and Eixarch, servants, muleteers, cattle drivers, families and soldiers the expedition numbered some 240 persons. Over one thousand domestic animals were taken including nearly 700 horses and mules and 350 beef cattle. The cattle were used for subsistence enroute and for the new settlements, particularly San Francisco. The Anza expedition nearly doubled the domestic animal population in Alta California (Bean 1973).

Father Pedro Font, acting in the capacity of chaplain and chronicler of the expedition left a journal full of information about Chumash customs and ethnography. He gave fine descriptions of Chumash dress and physiology saying they are "Well formed and of good body but not very fat on account of their sweating." He gave a detailed portrait of a Chumash sweat house, which the Spanish call *temescals*.

> "This is a hot, closed room for sweating, made somewhat subterranean and very firm with poles and earth, and having at the top, in the middle, an opening like a scuttle to afford air and to serve as a door through which they go down inside by a ladder consisting of straight poles set in the ground and joined together, one being shorter than the other...In the middle of them, they make a fire. The Indians enter to perspire, seated all around and as soon as they perspire freely and wet the ground with their sweat, they run out an jump into the sea" (Bolton 1930:250,254).

Fr. Font was a fearless observer and tended to be more frank than his contemporary Fr. Juan Crespí.

> "The men go entirely naked. For the sake of adornment only, they generally wear a girdle of fibers. On the head they tie up the hair in a sort of lump or crown. In this they fasten some little stick or feather, and especially a kind of knife, which is a thin blade of wood, about two fingers wide and about a foot long. On one end of it they tie and secure with pitch a somewhat large and sharp flint which has a double edge...Among the Indian men I saw a few with a kind of cape of bear skin. I understood that this was worn as a distinction by the owners of the canoes.
>
> The women cover themselves with deer skins hanging from the waist, with a cape of otter skins over the shoulders...and are pretty, and they have pendants in the ears. They wear the hair in front cut short and arranged like a toupe, while the rest hangs down over the shoulders" (Bolton 1931).

Fr. Font also noted that the women, particularly the young women, ran and hid when the Spanish approached. He laid this to the abuse they had suffered from the soldiers in the past.

The expedition ended on March 29, 1776 with the founding of the Mission

San Francisco de Asis by the side of a creek which Anza named *Laguna de Nuestra Senora de los Dolores* and from which the popular name Mission Dolores arose. This was the sixth in the chain of California missions that was slowly but surely being forged by the Spanish and that would become the shackles by which they bound the California Indian population. The Chumash, one of the largest Indian groups was far from exempt and they were shortly to find more missions sprouting in their midst (Bean 1973).

Between Mission San Luis Obispo and Mission San Gabriel there was a lot of territory and Father Serra proposed three new missions in this gap along the Santa Barbara Channel.

In 1782, Serra obtained permission to build the additional missions in Chumash territory. Consequently Mission San Buenaventura and the Presidio at Santa Barbara were founded. That day at the presidio the *Padre-Presidente* Serra, clad in alb and stole, stood before a rough wooden altar with a group of Chumash and 36 *soldados de cuera* (leather jacketed soldiers) and blessed the site. It would not be until four years later in 1786 the the actual mission at Santa Barbara was built some short distance away.

Further south the Mission San Buenaventura came into being at the mouth of the Ventura River. The Chumash in this area were numerous and easily pacified and so the mission thrived from the start. The Padres directed the building of a reservoir and an aqueduct system seven miles long to bring water to the mission fields. This was the last mission that Serra oversaw personally. He died in Carmel at the Mission San Carlos Borromeo on August 28th, 1784 at the age of 70, bitterly disappointed that he was not able to see the foundations raised at Santa Barbara. Father Francisco Palou gave him the last sacraments and in the afternoon he died. He was buried beside his companion Father Juan Crespí who had passed away several years before.

Serra's successor, *Padre Presidente* Fermin Lasuen, finally founded Mission Santa Barbara (called "Queen of the Missions") on December 4, 1786. This was the tenth mission in the chain and the third within Chumash territory. It was a stormy winter that year and the major building didn't begin until the spring when the temporary buildings were replaced with adobe structures. By year's end 1787, there were 185 neophytes converted from the large *rancheria*, (*Syuhtun*) nearby. Aqueducts were built to bring water from the Santa Ynez mountains that that formed a high backdrop behind the mission and as the water came, the fields were planted. In 1788 the original chapel was enlarged and the next year a large church with the traditional red adobe roof tiles was erected to make room for the ever increasing number of Chumash converts. The mission flock amounted to 428 souls at this time (Engelhardt 1923).

For the most part these converts were camped around the missions away from their traditional village sites. They were taught to abandon their pagan ways by the priests and learned the basic trades to establish the mission economy. They learned tilemaking, woodworking, agriculture, weaving, animal husbandry, metal forging and leather crafts. The women worked in the shops spinning, weaving and sewing; making everything from shirts to pantaloons. Moccasins and jackets were made of leather and blankets were woven of wool. The men dug the irrigation ditches, tended the crops, plowed the fields and built the buildings. Everyone did the harvesting of crops. They were not however, with few exceptions, taught to read beyond a few musical notes for fear that education would promote dissension and strife among them (Grant 1965).

The daily routine of the Indians was prescribed in detailed written regulations. The Indians were made to follow it unwaveringly. If they did not food was withheld or the lash applied. When girls reached the age of eleven they were kept with the other single women and with the women whose husbands had fled in the *monjerio* or nunnery that was locked each night.

At first light the bell was tolled and the all Indians over the age of nine were to appear at Divine Mass. After Mass the Indians were instructed in the Spanish language and then released for breakfast. Unattached men and women were not allowed to eat together but had to go to their respective quarters.

The mission industry and economy was kept up by the native labor. With the profits from selling products to the presidios, settlers, and Yankee traders, the priests bought metals, primarily iron, as well as cloth and tools. Some profits went to embellishments for the mission chapels, statues, religious goods, crucifixes and occasionally trinkets for the Indians.

Each year the mission fathers appointed an Indian *alcaldes*. These *alcaldes* were not necessarily chosen from the elite Chumash and hence owed their new found power to the priests and not the traditional Chumash elders. Thus one more way was found to enhance the mission system: alter the power base and a new group benefits while the old erodes.

The missions were meant to be self sustaining, and a complete new life for the neophytes. They provided the men with a pair a breeches and shirt or for the women a skirt. In return the Indians were made to build the presidios and missions, including the nine foot walls that surrounded them at night.

By 1799, at the Santa Barbara Mission the Chumash had built a large church, six chapels that stood alongside, a granary, a jail, a quadrangle surrounding the entire mission area with walls eight and one half feet tall and measuring 3300 feet in length, and nineteen adobe walled, tile roofed houses nearby for themselves. In addition thirty-one houses of the same type were built on the site of their old village to accommodate the new converts. By the end of the year the Death Register at the Santa Barbara Mission had 736 entries (Engelhardt 1923).

Lacking immunity to European diseases, such as tuberculosis, chicken pox, measles, smallpox, and syphilis, the Chumash were swept with epidemics. Their numbers dwindled. The average lifespan of a neophyte was perhaps six or seven years and even then there was a 40% chance of dying. They died of European enlightenment — hard work, diseases, and an unaccustomed diet.

In 1801, pneumonia and other diseases were rampant, infecting and killing large numbers of the Chumash, creating the worst epidemic yet. This same year the first signs of an organized rebellion among the Chumash commenced. One night a young neophyte woman went into a trance and received a vision. A Chumash religious leader interpreted the vision saying that an offering must be made to the native God Chupu and all neophytes must renounce their Christian beliefs. News of this vision spread rapidly but to no avail. Within three days the Padres had squelched the revolt before it was really underway. Still the sudden upswelling of dissent and the speed at which it spread alarmed the priests (Sandos 1987).

Mission life continued as before with little respite for the Chumash and the surprising thing is that even with the high death rate the Indian population around the missions continued to expand. In fact the population for the entire mission chain was set in 1803 at 20,000, the highest it ever became. That year the Santa Barbara mission celebrated Mass with nearly 1800 Indians, the largest number before or after.

A system of peonage was established at the missions. The Indians were farmed out to the soldiers or settlers to do what ever work was needed and in return the mission was paid. This newly trained work force was extremely valuable to the mission fathers and they would not have been able to succeed had the Indians resisted.

Father Ramon Olbes, in answering one of the questionnaires (*Interrogatorios*) sent to the missions by the Spanish authorities in Mexico observed:

> "The people in this province, known as the *gente de razon*, (people of reason-whites), are so lazy and indolent that they know nothing more than how to ride horseback. Labor of any kind they regard as dishonorable. They are of the opinion that only the Indians ought to work; wherefore they solicit the service of the Indians for even the most necessary things for their maintenance such as cooking, washing, doing garden work, taking care of babies, etc. Generally the missionary Fathers let them have the Indians for work" (Engelhardt 1923:98).

The responses (*respuestas*) which the Fathers made to the thirty six questions put to them by the Spanish Government are illuminating in some respects and contain interesting information about the Chumash. The mission fathers themselves although no doubt good observers of human nature, had little interest in any ethnographic reporting. Hence much of what could have been observed and recorded has been lost forever. Nevertheless there are a good many diaries, journals and *interrogatorio* of various sorts, made by the priests, yankee traders, and civil and military authorities. These provide a window by which one gets an imperfect view of the Chumash: a sort of historical glimpse full of natural bias but nonetheless an honest account from the diarist's perspective. So in absence of better sources these must do.

From the turn of the century on the mistreatment of the Chumash neophytes increased both in frequency and severity. Thus it was not surprising that on the afternoon of February 21, 1824, at Santa Ynez at around two or three o'clock the Chumash neophytes revolted, burning the mission and the soldiers' quarters. Two Chumash were killed during this battle but the Indians spared the priest, Father Uria. The revolt which had been simmering awhile was touched off by the flogging of one of the neophytes. A comet had recently appeared in the night sky over southern California and to the Chumash, who were aware of the sky, this was a powerful symbol that signified a change or a new beginning. On that Saturday afternoon it began (Sandos 1987).

Later that same day, Indians at La Purísima Concepción, hearing of the uprising at Santa Ynez, armed themselves with bows and arrows and took over the mission after the six soldiers there surrendered. This battle was short and only one Indian was killed but four travelers who were on their way to Los Angeles were murdered by the aroused neophytes.

It was a full month before more than 100 soldiers came and demanded the surrender of the La Purísima Indians. They failed until Father Antonio Rodriquez convinced the rebellious neophytes to cease and desist but not before 16 were killed and many wounded. On the Mexican side one soldier was dead and two were wounded. The soldiers took retribution for the revolt by executing seven Indians and sentencing twelve to long imprisonment (Grant 1965).

At Santa Barbara the revolt started somewhat less intensely but was exacerbated by the insolent military stationed at the Presidio. The Santa Barbara neophytes afraid that the Presidio troops would attack and kill them during Mass, started to arm themselves, mostly with bows and arrows and a half a dozen guns from the storerooms.

At this time the Chumash at the mission numbered around a thousand about half of which were women, who did not take up weapons. Neither did about two fifths of the males who were under the age of eighteen and who fled with their mothers up Mission Creek. This left about 300 fighting men some of whom were aged.

There was a pitched battle for three hours at the mission which ended in a standoff when Captain Jose De la Guerra and his troops retired to the Presidio. The Indians found themselves still in possession of the mission and grounds. In all, four troops had been wounded as well as three Indians one of whom died the next day, making the total dead on the Indian side at three. The next day the Indians retreated to the Sierra Madre (Engelhardt 1923).

Father Ripoll gave an account of February 22, 1824 at the Mission Santa Barbara.

> "On learning that the mission had been deserted, the comman-
> dante sent up about ten soldiers. They encountered no one but a
> half witted Indian in one of the houses without being guilty of any
> crime, he was kept in prison two or three months, as were four or
> five aged women. The soldiers then went around the houses, and
> near the threshing ground they met one Indian, who, mounted
> on a mule was carrying away a quantity of wheat in a blanket.
> They seized him and shot him dead!
> On the following day another squad of soldiers was ordered
> out. When they came near the corral, they met four old wander-
> ing Indians from Dos Pueblos, who neither knew the people, nor
> had been in the tumult, nor had done anything amiss. Because
> they had heard there was trouble at the Mission they had come to
> see what it was about. The soldiers descried them, fell upon them,
> and killed all four" (Engelhardt 1923:128).

That day the soldiers also sacked the deserted Indian dwellings. Meanwhile the Indian fugitives from the Mission Santa Barbara, seeing what had happened to the four Indians from Dos Pueblos and the ruins of their houses, would not return. They had already moved their camp from the Mission Creek to a higher spot in the Sierra and now they fled further inland to the *Tulares* in the San Joaquin Valley where they joined fugitives from Santa Ynez and La Purísima.

Captain De la Guerra knew full well that the mission system and the Presidio could not survive without the Indians so he ordered Lieutenant Narciso Fabregat and eighty men to overtake the fugitives and bring them back forceably. Fabregat caught them on April 9, near Buena Vista Lake in Kern county and had a brief skirmish. The Indians fled again this time to the San Emigdio hills where Fabregat and Sergeant Carlos Carrillo attacked and killed four Indians. Thinking that victory had been served Fabregat led his men back to Santa Barbara (Grant 1965).

Governor Arguello and Commandante De la Guerra were not pleased and

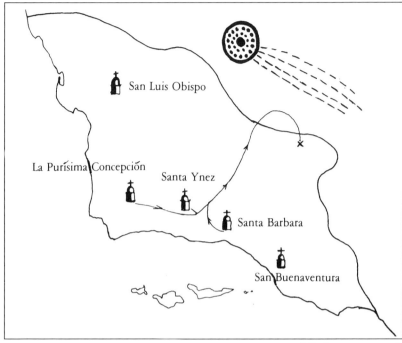

Direction of flight in 1824 revolt.

were determined to bring the Chumash fugitives back.

On June 2nd another expedition consisting of sixty-three soldiers from the Presidio and commanded by Captain Pablo de la Portilla set out from Santa Barbara. These men, along with sixty soldiers from Monterey converged on the Indians who were still in the San Emigdio hills. Both military groups had cannon and were prepared for full battle. This did not come about, primarily because of the mitigating presence of Father Sarria from the Mission Santa Barbara who had been persuaded to come along; he had refused to join Fabregat's expedition. He reasoned that some bloodshed might be saved if he could persuade the Indians to come back freely with a full pardon. Captain Portilla carried that pardon from the Governor with him. Both groups met and had council but still the Indians feared retribution if they laid down their arms. They knew of course that the La Purísima fugitives had not fared very well.

In a surprising turnabout the Reverend Father Vicente de Sarria, with Father Ripoll at his side, convinced the Indians to return to the mission. Some of the Chumash, more than a third, did not return but settled in the San Joaquin Valley. However, some of the Valley Yokut Indians came back to the

Santa Barbara mission. Thus this somewhat abortive revolt was ended on a peaceful note. The Indians were not given any reparation for the destruction of their houses nor were the soldiers punished (Sandos 1987).

That same year (1824) Mexico declared itself free of Spain and the liberal minded new government framed the Federal Constitution of the United Mexican States modelling their document after the Constitution of the United States.

One of the first notions the new government put into practice was the secularization of the missions. In 1827 the Indians were declared free and able to move at will. Having been taught domestic skills by the mission Fathers, they were to go out and put these skills into practice and become useful citizens of the new republic. The mission Fathers argued against secularization because it would bring the vast mission lands under control of the government. The five missions within the Chumash territory had large land holdings, on which well over 150,000 cattle, 60,000 sheep and thousands of horses and mules grazed (Davis 1929:389).

It was also argued that the Indians were not ready for secularization. Some countered that after fifty years under the mission system they would never be ready.

Full secularization of the missions, which began in 1833 meant a dramatic change for the California Indians and the Mission fathers. Private citizens were now given land grants over the territory previously controlled by the missions (Grant 1965).

The terms of the secularization in Governor Jose Figueroa's Provisional Regulation for the Emancipation of the Mission Indians issued July 15, 1833, were that half the land and property of the missions was to go to the Indians and half to the administrators. Many of these administrators were unscrupulous or at the very least lacking in conscience and ability to hold the property in trust for the Indians. The law forbade the Indians from disposing of their land so many tried farming small plots for a few years but they quickly failed and gave up the effort. Some were dispossessed by trick or by debt and the mission lands fell into the hands of those holding land grants or were subdivided into ranchos (Bean 1973).

Secularization didn't change the demands made on the Chumash: the Presidio at Santa Barbara still insisted on work without recompense. By 1839 there were 246 Indians living at the Santa Barbara Mission and its vicinity. Thus, in six decades, the space of a single lifetime, the Chumash nation whose territory stretched over 7,000 square miles and whose people numbered many thousands had been reduced to near extinction. Culturally and spiritually they had very nearly ceased to exist (Grant 1965).

AFTERMATH

AS THE MISSIONS died the Chumash were scattered to the wind. Dispossessed of their traditional hunting lands and old village sites along the coast the Chumash huddled around the remnants of the missions, or went to work on the vast ranchos as stock men and domestic servants. Some drifted inland to join the interior tribes. In every case however, their old life was finished, the missions had changed that indelibly and forever. Stripped of their heritage and many of their beliefs abandoned, they had been culturally overwhelmed. The Chumash believed they had lost control of their universe and there were few shamans around to help right it. The old ways of hunting and gathering were lost, the Chumash leaders, what few were left, were virtually underground, fearful of public scrutiny. The special language and ceremonial rituals of these persons of power had slipped into obsolescence. The meaning of things Chumash — actions, rock paintings, words, mythology, symbology faded or were adulterated with Spanish and American ways.

Families were separated, tribal life was discouraged and Indians who sought the old ways were intimidated by constant harassment. The social structure of the Chumash villages, the family, the craft guilds, and the ruling elite that had been relatively intact even though the villages had been deserted during mission times, broke down completely now, as the Indians were further divided and absorbed by the Spanish settlements.

In the absence of their own culture the Indians adopted the life of the rancho. Clearly the Chumash fared no better in their freedom than they had under the bondage of the mission system. They had merely changed masters from religious to secular, from mission to rancho (Grant 1965).

Drastic changes had to be reckoned with, the Chumash struggled to survive and worked and lived where they could. The ranchos provided some refuge if hard work. In return for their labor they received food and shelter but little else. A once proud, rich and peaceful Indian nation, culturally and linguistically diverse had been reduced by civilization to a dispirited and lost group of illiterate christian laborers, no longer in control of their destiny (Margolin 1978).

California was rapidly changing and the ranchos were a sign of that change. This was the flowering of Mexican influence in California and for the land grant Mexicans, the *Hacendados*, life was bountiful and easy on their vast acreage. Time was spent herding and raising cattle and sheep, on annual roundups (*rodeo*), on branding and marketing hides and tallow from their livestock. Hides were simply staked out to stretch-dry in the sun, while the tallow was being rendered, reduced and then placed in *botas* made out of several whole hides sewn together. Barbecues, *fiesta*, bull and bear baiting, horsemanship, cockfighting and landed politics were the activities of the *rancheros*. The favorite dances were the *jota*, the *bamba* and the *fandango*. The ranchos, much like feudal kingdoms, were far from self-sufficient however, in fact much of what had been accomplished under the missions in terms of agriculture and domestic arts was lost during secularization. Some was lost due to deliberate destruction by the priests who did not want to see their hard work fall into the hands of others and some by neglect and laziness of the *rancheros*. Formerly the missions had made coarse woolen blankets, shoes, saddles, soap, candles and other basics supplies. Now much of this was done in New England and or in the Spanish settlements of Chile and Peru (Dana 1937), (Grant 1965).

Where the mission economy had produced a variety of agricultural products by the use of irrigation—wheat, barley, numerous fruits and fresh vegetables, pumpkins, olives, muskmelons and grapes, the ranchos imported from Yankee traders many basic necessities. On the ranchos, diet was beef—fresh, barbecued, and jerked. Fresh milk, wheat flour, sugar, and molasses were used infrequently and considered luxuries. However, not withstanding the relative laziness and lack of industry on these sprawling ranchos, the owners and overlords did quite well (Bean 1973).

Though greatly romanticized, these *"halcyon days of the dons"* were just another trial to the Chumash. The Indians worked and survived and adapted as best they could under harsh circumstances. Living in extreme poverty, they were still abused and despised especially by the whites, the American settlers (*gringos*), who were slowly infiltrating Mexican California.

Though the Chumash were perhaps only 10% of their original number they started to increase slowly, mainly through intermarriage with the Spanish and Mexican counterparts. In some ways the time of the *rancheros* in California may have helped to stabilized the Indian death rate. While the pure blood Chumash continued to decrease for the next few generations those Chumash who were forced to adapt at the cost of their culture, survived. Their culture, language and subsistence way of life were dying but the people remained.

During the mission days they had been allowed to leave the missions for short durations to continue foraging for food, to hunt and to visit their *rancherías*. This no doubt contributed somewhat to the continuation of their culture. But increasingly these villages ceased to exist and the Chumash were culturally bereft. The Island Chumash had long since disappeared, killed by Russian whalers and their Aleut harpoonists or had been rounded up by the padres and brought to the mainland missions. A few had tried to repopulate Santa Cruz Island during the revolt of 1824, but had quickly faltered and returned to the mainland (Sandos 1987).

It was a grim time for the Chumash, a sort of vale of tears as they were assimilated into a foreign culture. They learned to speak Spanish and later English and forgot the Hokan dialects they had spoken for centuries. Gone were their *temescals*, their games, beliefs and their prosperous way of life (McCall & Perry 1982).

In 1834 Zenas Leonard, a fur trapper traveling in service as a clerk with Joseph Reddeford Walker's expedition made some interesting observations on local Indian life. The expedition was exploring a continental passage from Missouri westward. They came through the Sierras with the loss of many pack animals and they were probably the first white men to see the magnificent Yosemite Valley. Coming down the central valley from Monterey they found 700 Chumash who spoke Spanish and farmed the land. These were the neophytes that had fled during the mission uprising in 1824. They had been joined by other fugitives and prospered on their own with a cultural mixture of Spanish and traditional ways (Grant 1965).

The renegade Chumash and Yokuts had survived and even became stronger having learned the art of horsemanship and subsistence agriculture. They continually raided the eastern edge of the ranchos, stealing cattle and horses, a crime for which the *rancheros* often exacted a terrible punishment.

It is thought that with the aid of the Sierra Indians the Mexicans would have eventually been overwhelmed if it were not for the sudden and dramatic influx of Americans during the Gold Rush and a dreadful malaria epidemic that killed many Indians when it swept the Central Valley in the early 1830's (Kirsch & Murphy 1967).

The gold rush was an event which changed everything and sounded an ominous final toll for the pure blood Chumash. All the California Indians suffered during this time when more than fifty thousand California Indians were slaughtered in two short years. The mission Indians were seen by the whites as a dispirited and impoverished lot and were called "diggers". The Americans largely ignored them or placed them on reservations (Heizer 1974).

A Chumash reservation was established at Tejon Pass in 1854, not far from where the notorious bandit Joaquin Murrieta had been run to ground and killed a few years earlier. The reservation proved untenable for a number of reasons, including a disparate mixture of Indian tribes, lack of leadership, theft, and poor planning. It quickly deteriorated and the Indians dispersed. Another small group of mixed blood Chumash lived around the remnants of the Santa Ynez Mission and continue to do so today. It is now called the Santa Ynez Chumash Reservation (Grant 1965).

The Chumash who fled to the interior suffered constant harassment and they along with most of the non-Christianized California Indians, the Yokuts and Valley Indians, were wiped out, dispersed or had intermarried by the 1890's: such that these fugitive Chumash no longer constituted the dynamics of their own culture. By the turn of the century there were only a handful of pure blood Chumash living. Presently there are some 1500 people of Chumash descent living in the San Luis Obispo, Santa Barbara, and Ventura counties.

John Peabody Harrington (left), David Banks Rogers (center) and unidentified figure at Burton Mound, 1924. Burton Mound was the site of a major Chumash village in Santa Barbara, excavated by Harrington and Rogers in 1923 for the Smithsonian Institute. Courtesy of the Smithsonian Institution.

During the early years of this century an anthropologist named John Peabody Harrington collected a great deal of information on the Chumash. Some of his native informants, and there were many, most notably Fernando Librado *Kipsepawit* and Maria Solares, had themselves sought out many aspects of their own culture. Because of these native informants we are now able to know much that would have been lost. Surely our understanding owes a tremendous debt to their efforts. Presently the Harrington material, a trove of some one thousand boxes of notes many of which concern the Chumash, is in the Smithsonian Institution. What it will yield has only recently started to see the light with such publications of The Santa Barbara Museum of Natural History as *Crystals in the Sky* on Chumash archaeoastronomy, *The Eye of the Flute* on the traditional festivals and rituals, and *The Material Culture of the Chumash Interaction Sphere*, a massive five volume set on material culture. Another book based on the Harrington material is *December's Child, A Book of Chumash Oral Narratives*, by Thomas C. Blackburn. These titles and others form the backbone of present day Chumash research.

.

MATERIAL CULTURE

CAPTURED HERITAGE

IN THE 1870's an intense interest in the Chumash developed. This intensity was not directed at the living people but towards the relics and buried artifacts of their fading culture nor was it exclusive to the Chumash nation. The great museums of the world were starting to build their collections and the race was on. Everywhere along the coast of North America the Indian heritage was being crated up and shipped out to the four corners. Collections of Chumash relics reside not only in the major American institutions but in such places as Moscow, and Madrid, in Paris at the Musée de L'Homme and in London at the British Museum. In part this acquisitive mania was a sign of the times. The Victorians were great collectors every type of object from Polynesian masks to Chumash basketry. Spurred on by the Darwinian revolution every primitive culture around the world felt the clutching hand of civilized man.

As it happened in the years following 1873, three different groups of archaeologists, itinerant and otherwise, converged on the Santa Barbara Channel area. The first to arrive was an expedition headed by Paul Schumacher under the greater auspices of the Smithsonian Institution and the Peabody Museum. Shortly thereafter Dr. Harry Crecy Yarrow arrived with the U.S. Army Engineer Corps, who were doing a geographical survey west of the 100th meridian. Schumacher and Yarrow agreed to divide their efforts and the territory. Yarrow started digging on the mainland and Schumacher undertook to investigate the Santa Barbara Channel Islands. The third party, considered interlopers by Schumacher, was a French scientific expedition financed and headed by Alphonse Pinart but undertaken at the instigation of Leon de Cessac, a scientist known for his studies in physiography and volcanic phenomena (Grant 1965:25).

The stakes were high, personal reputations rested on the ability to find and control certain sites and the digging paid off handsomely. The Yarrow party, for example, removed as much as fifteen tons of artifacts from mainland sites.

Leon de Cessac speaks of circumventing Schumacher's restrictions on the Burton Mound, a particularly rich trove of archaeological artifacts with a liberal use of "money, discretion and whiskey" (Grant 1965:26).

These and many others to follow, set the shovels digging and the dirt flying. Unfortunately not many of these people had the slightest scientific training or concern for the sites they were pillaging. Hence much of what might have been learned was lost. Anthropology of course was not an accepted science until the 1890's but this alone cannot account for the wanton destruction of so many sites.

Schumacher worked in the Santa Barbara area during the years of 1873—1880 excavating a major collection for the Smithsonian. He was responsible for the removal of massive amounts of archaeological material from the area. During this time he published some of the earliest reports on the archaeology of California including studies on ancient graves, settlements, shell heaps, and the manufacture of pottery and baskets. Here is an excerpt from his report of 1877.

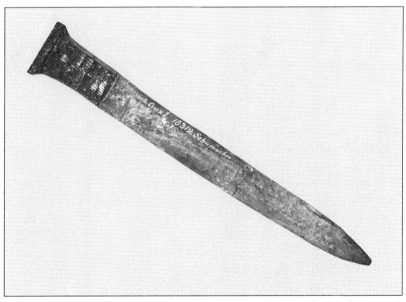

Wooden ceremonial wand inlaid with pieces of shell, excavated by Paul Schumacher on Santa Cruz Island in 1876. Courtesy of the Smithsonian Institution.

"The skeletons were found from three to six feet underground and often from three to four resting above one another, separated if at all by the bones of the whale. The bodies were deposited without any order as to position and direction of the face being sometimes found face downward, lying on one side, or in the back, or face to face, or crosswise, and in nine times out of ten disturbed and displaced...It is evident that the burial took place before the decay of the body, although such was not the custom of some interior tribes, because we found bones of some of the skeletons buried deepest, and especially such as were interred separately from the others in perfect order. Some were even still enwrapped in matting. To a find skeleton at the bottom of a pit, at the depth of five or six feet, especially if there be none above it, is considered by the practical digger a lucky hit, and causes him to work carefully in the removal of slabs and whalebones, and to look for stone knives, spear points or strange stone implements, as it is supposed to be either the grave of a warrior, a chief, or a *medicine man*."

Schumacher was stiff competition for Leon de Cessac who had set up operations on Santa Cruz Island, then under the control of a French wool company. First he told de Cessac that it was against the law to remove archaeological objects from the continental United States to a foreign country and he got the local authorities to back him up, threatening to confiscate any artifact collections. Then he used his influence to persuade the Secretary of the Smithsonian Institution to have Congress pass an act forbidding the exportation of prehistoric objects. The Secretary declined to approach the Senate and the matter was closed.

Realizing that there was nothing to stop him, de Cessac continued digging. His operations had barely started again when his patron Alphonse Pinart informed that the inheritance which was funding the expedition was gone, and that he would no longer be able to finance further excavations. De Cessac took this news in stride and continued his work for nearly a year until his own sources of money, mainly borrowed funds dried up. In that time he amassed a stunning collection of over 3000 artifacts now in the Musée de l'Homme in Paris.

The highlights of the de Cessac collections include a series of flint burins found on Santa Cruz Island generally associated with the Upper Paleolithic era in Europe. The presence of this type of burin has only been known in the Americas for the last twenty years. He also collected from the Santa Ynez Valley two wonderful wooden bowls worked from oak to a fine smoothness and shaped in the fashion of Pre-Columbian steatite mortars with the rim inlaid with pieces of shell. From San Nicolas Island he put together a remarkable collection of steatite effigies that resemble sea birds (Reichlen & Heizer:1963).

Raphael Solares one of the last 'antap. 1877.
Solares demonstrates the use of self bow.
Note: body paint, top knot headdress and
down cord skirt. Photograph by Leon
de Cessac. Courtesy Musée de l'Homme.

MATERIAL CULTURE

WHAT THEY MADE

FROM THE ARCHAEOLOGICAL evidence and earliest historical sources it is clear that the Chumash were the very finest of craftsmen. They excelled in many areas, basketry, tool making, rock art, and boat building to name the most obvious. They were great users of materials at hand and exercised a wide trading partnership with nearby groups for those materials they couldn't get locally. They used sandstone, steatite, wood, grass, animal hides, seashells, bones, chert, asphaltum, and just about anything else that was serviceable in their environment.

Much of what the Chumash people used has not survived today, with the exception of those things made of stone, shell and bone. For the most part the perishable items such as baskets are in museums and private collections and date from the mission period. Other woven or feathered artifacts, head-dresses, skirts, and fish nets are fewer and very scarce. The majority of wooden artifacts, bowls, mortars, bows and arrows, and canoes have perished with only a few exceptions. Nevertheless, those artifacts extant demonstrate the rich and varied life the Chumash led.

Much of the archaeological work on Chumash material culture has centered on those village sites perched along the coastal plain of the Santa Barbara Channel. Past work suggests that this area had the most complex cultural heritage within Chumash territory. The Santa Barbara Channel area reached a peak primarily because of the relatively bountiful landscape, which in turn led to permanent and larger villages where cultural activities thrived. It should be noted that some recent studies partially discount this conclusion suggesting there was a great deal of homogeneity in material culture throughout the whole region.

The life of the Chumash was centered around the household and in turn the village with much of the daily activity performed there. Their material culture certainly reflects these various activities. Food was brought to the village site to be prepared and then consumed with the excess put into storage. The Chumash built large thatched dwellings occupied by extended family groups with as many as forty or fifty people living in one structure. In the larger villages the houses were well kept even though made of relatively perishable materials and they were placed in neat rows with streets in between. Inside, the house was spacious and comfortable with light entering through a hole in the roof. Reed mats were hung from the ceiling as curtains to make a partitioned room. More woven tule was laid on top of rushes that filled the raised beds to make a mattress. Pillows and blankets were made from woven fur or hides.

When not spending time on hunting, gathering and food preparation the Chumash were playing games; they were inveterate gamblers. Preparing for rituals and celebrations, putting on body paint, observing traditional behavior and making personal adornments were common activities. Each of these aspects of Chumash lifeways had its own variety of sophisticated material culture and contributed to the richness of the Indians' lives. It is no wonder that they were a peaceful and happy people.

BASKETRY

THE CHUMASH WERE superb basket makers. So beautifully wrought were these baskets that the Spanish explorers and settlers avidly collected them for their own use. There are many historical accounts which attest to the variety and intricacy of Chumash basketry and to the many uses the Indians made of them. Father Pedro Font on the Anza expedition wrote in his diary that there was barter and trade for Chumash baskets in nearly every village encountered.

Baskets were indispensable in the daily life of the Chumash. They were used in every aspect of food preparation from collecting roots, bulbs and other foodstuffs, to carrying or storing water. They were used as plates and bowls for serving, as seed beaters, as containers for straining, leaching, cooking and storing food, for carrying large burdens, for fishing, for gambling, for storing small trinkets and precious ritual objects, for use in the rituals themselves and in historical times as presentation gifts to important persons.

The basket weavers used two basic methods, coiling and twining. The coiled ware included baskets for food preparation, seed storage and trays, bucket and basin shaped baskets, burden and trinket baskets and women's basketry hats. The twined ware was used for fishing, seed beating, straining, leaching, and water storage.

A third type distinct from the first two and perhaps less common was the wicker woven basket. Two wicker seed beaters found in storage caves have come to light consisting of flat bent wooden slats bound to a Y-forked handle.

The Chumash lived in a relatively dry climate (particularly the Inland and Island Chumash) where scarce water supplies made the ability to store water an absolute necessity. Presented with this need they developed an ingenious method for making watertight baskets. Many baskets, especially twined baskets, were extremely fine and so tightly woven that they held water on their own even though they weren't meant for liquid storage. To solve the problem of long term water storage the Chumash would line the inside of a basket

Basket tray collected by Malaspina Expedition
1791. Photograph: Arthur Taylor,
Courtesy Museo de America, Museum of
New Mexico.

Small Basket tray. Coiled winnower used for
sifting and separating seeds from the chaff.
Courtesy of the Ventura County
Historical Museum.

Globular trinket basket. Courtesy of the
Smithsonian Institution.

Silhouettes of large and small water storage
basket bottles. They were twined baskets sealed
with asphaltum inside and out.

with asphaltum (tar that seeped from underground deposits). These water storage baskets could be the size of a small water bottle or quite large holding five or six gallons. They were twined from rush or tule and were rougher in appearance than most coiled wear and generally very plain with little or no decoration.

George Nidever, a fur trapper, recorded the process of lining a water storage basket with asphaltum that he witnessed on San Nicolas Island as performed by the "Lone Woman."

> "She had built a fire and had several small stones about the size of a walnut heating in it. Taking one of the vessels, which was in shape and size very like a demi-john, excepting that the neck and mouth were much longer, she dropped a few pieces of asphaltum within it and as soon as the stones were well heated they were dropped in on top of the asphaltum. They soon melted it, when, resting on the bottom of the vessel on the ground, she gave it a rotary motion with both hands until the interior was completely covered with asphaltum. These vessels hold water well, and if kept full may be placed with safety in a hot sun" (Nidever 1973:14).

For storage of dry materials, grain, acorns and such, the Chumash made large coiled baskets that were elevated on a rack-like platform of poles. These storage baskets were sometimes covered with asphaltum on the outside. Having no lid, the large opening on the top was covered with another basket and weighted with a stone. These plainly designed juncus baskets were purely utilitarian. Sometimes ceremonial regalia was stored in these large granaries.

Basketry bowls were used for serving food and for standard measures of seeds offered in trade. They are coiled, fairly large and somewhat shallow. There are two major types: the first is in the shape of a wide basin with a rounded base and gently curved and flared sides; the second resembles a foreshortened cone with a flat base and rather straight flaring sides.

Basket dishes are held in the palm of the hand and used for serving individual portions. They are similar in design and shape to the basket bowls but smaller in size.

The Chumash made many kinds of trays, small and large coiled winnowers, basket trays for serving food, parching and leaching trays, and gambling trays. These trays were generally the same shape, nearly flat, with very finely woven coil designs. The exception was the leaching tray which was twined. The same tray may have had multiple purposes, being used for serving food and then later for gambling.

The winnowing trays ranged in size from a large hand spread to very large, perhaps a meter in diameter. They were used to separate chaff from chia seeds

*Basket dish. The pedestal base may be a non-
Chumash design feature, possibly European
(Dawson & Deetz 1965).
Courtesy of the Smithsonian Institute.*

*Basket bowl. Courtesy The Nelson-Atkins
Museum of Art, Kansas City, Missouri
(Nelson Fund).*

Chumash basket bowl collected by Malaspina Expedition 1791. Stair step block cascades fill the body zone in this basket. Photograph: Arthur Taylor, courtesy Museo de America, Museum of New Mexico.

Basket bowl collected in the Santa Barbara area by Vancouver in 1793. Note the alternating black and white rim ticks a common design element in Chumash basketry. Diameter 45 cm. Courtesy of the British Museum.

Chumash basket bowl collected by Malaspina Expedition 1791. In this piece the block cascade fills the principal band and then descends in a spiral to the base zone. Photograph: Arthur Taylor, courtesy Museo de America, Museum of New Mexico.

Basket bowl collected in the Santa Barbara area by Vancouver in 1793. Diameter 30 cm. Courtesy of the British Museum.

and for sifting acorn meal. Parching trays were about twenty inches in diameter and sometimes had the interior covered with asphaltum. They were used for drying seeds (Hudson & Blackburn 1983).

The basket hopper mortar is an example of the often ingenious use the Chumash made of their basketry. A coiled bottomless basket was affixed with asphaltum to a mortar and in this fashion the seeds or vegetables being pulverized were contained on the grinding surface.

Some of the most beautiful baskets the Chumash made were not for food uses but for storing small ritual objects, money and jewelry. These were the wonderfully made globular and bottleneck trinket baskets. These small highly decorated coiled baskets were ellipsoidal in shape with a narrow opening. Some examples have a snugly fitting lid. They were generally quite small, never more than a foot in diameter and have about 180 stitches per square inch (Dawson & Deetz 1965).

The Chumash used a variety of basketry materials, most was which was found locally. Willow was found in wet areas near the rivers and natural springs. Rush, cattail, and tule were harvested in the esteros and small ponds. They were spread on the bank and left to dry and then separated and bundled for later use. Grass (*Epicampes regins*) was gathered in the summer.

Basket hopper mortar. Note the asphaltum
used to connect the basket to the mortar base.
Photograph courtesy of Museum of the
American Indian, Heye Foundation.

*Globular trinket basket collected by Malaspina
Expedition 1791. Precious objects and small
household tools were stored in these baskets.
Photograph: Arthur Taylor, courtesy Museo
de America, Museum of New Mexico.*

Bundles of rush (*Juncus balticus*) or deer grass (*Muhlenbergia rigens*) were used for coil foundations. For the wrapping and design, split *Juncus textilis* was common, giving the basket a natural straw or tan color or even black when the strands were buried in mud. Split peeled sumac shoots (*Rhus trilobata*) was used for white design elements, bracken fern root for black. Willow, sumac and tule were used for twining. Of all of these materials *Juncus* is by far the most prevalent.

The designs are sometimes quite complex though primarily geometric. Some principle characteristics of these beautiful pieces are that the work direction of the coiling moves from left to right, this being typical of all southern California tribes: that the fag ends are trimmed close to the work face, and that a both non-interlocking and interlocking stitch types are used. Occasionally the basket maker would incorporate olivella beads, quail and woodpecker feathers in the design elements (Dawson & Deetz 1965).

It is thought that the Chumash had a very explicit system of rules and design standards governing basket making. Probably every type of basket and every design element had some meaning that has now been lost to us. This was true of some tribes in California and elsewhere. In California in general, basket making was a high point of material culture. The Chumash were no exception.

*Bottleneck trinket basket collected by
Malaspina Expedition 1791. Used for storing
shell bead money. The flat top on this basket
may be a Yokut design feature. Photograph:
Arthur Taylor, Courtesy Museo de America,
Museum of New Mexico.*

*Basket box collected by Malaspina Expedition
1791. This specimen has a tightly fitting lid,
(not shown here). Photograph: Arthur Taylor,
Courtesy Museo de America, Museum of
New Mexico.*

WOODEN BOWLS AND JARS

THE WOODEN OBJECTS and dishes the Chumash left are quite extraordinary. They are all handworked, some are smeared with red ochre and polished to a dull lustrous sheen and the best of them have a fineness and definition that is unparalleled even in our own day.

There are some historical accounts of finely made wooden jars, even wooden boxes made of short planks sewn together and sealed with asphaltum. Costansó the engineer with the Portolá expedition noted:

> "The men make beautiful bowls of wood with solid inlays of shell or bone, and some vessels of great capacity, contracted at the mouth, which appear as if turned in a lathe, in fact, with this machine they could not be turned out better hollowed or more perfectly formed" (Hemert-Engert and Teggart 1910:45).

These bowls and jars ranged in size from a foot up to two and half feet with walls about a quarter of and inch thick. The bowls were used for serving, the jars for storage, and the mortars for grinding chia seeds and acorn meal. Some had tight fitted wooden lids. The preferred wood types for making them were oak burls, sycamore tree roots.

Other wooden implements and utensils include ladles, spoons, dishes, trays, cups, lifting sticks, and mashing paddles. These functional wooden items were made of willow, toyon, redwood, and cottonwood as suited the craftsman's needs and resources.

The Chumash had three basic steps to making these bowls. First came the selection of the wood, then shaping and hollowing and finally the decorating and polishing. The wood was worked into the desired shape immediately after cutting while still green, first being shaped and then hollowed. They may have been shaped by controlled burning of excess wood and then grinding away the charcoal to leave fresh wood. When finished the the wooden bowl or

*Wooden Jar collected by Leon de Cessac. This
finely made specimen is probably oak; note the
inlay of shell beads around the rim.
Courtesy Musée de l'Homme.*

jar would be dry polished and then a mixture of animal fat and red ochre was
smeared inside and out to seal the wood. Finally the bowl was left to dry in the
sun. After drying the bowl was polished again to a fine sheen. Some
specimens have the edge of the rim hollowed and inlaid with shell and
asphaltum (Hudson & Blackburn 1981:248).

Unfortunately very few of them survive today. Several marvelous examples
were collected in the Santa Ynez Valley in the late 1870's by Leon de Cessac
and are now in the Musée de L'Homme in Paris.

MATERIAL CULTURE

MORTARS, PESTLES, & OTHER STONE TOOLS

FOR THE TEN thousand years that the Chumash and their predecessors occupied the California coast, various kinds of stone implements were used. Over the years the style and shape of these tools changed. Sandstone, which was quite commonly available was the rock of choice to make metates, manos, mortars, bowls and pestles. Basaltic rock and granite were also used but much less frequently. Bedrock mortars were made on sandstone rock outcroppings. Light gray steatite came from Catalina Island where it was mined in numerous quarries by the Gabrielinos. It was used for cooking pots and other implements that would be subjected to heat. It was from serpentine that they made their most beautiful objects, charmstones, pipes, ritual bowls, effigies and ornaments. Knives, scrapers, drills and projectile points were made from chert, flint and obsidian. Flint and obsidian were obtained in trade size chunks from the southeastern tribes.

Mortars and pestles, used by the Indians to pulverize vegetable food, seeds and occasionally meat were made by chipping away at a large round piece of sandstone. A pestle usually made of sandstone was the grinding implement that accompanied the mortar. Harrington noted that...

> "Pestles lend themselves nicely to classification. There are the extra long, the ordinary, and the short and chubby. Some are little more than natural stones, others beautifully symmetrical in their workmanship. Some were flanged at the tip end to give a better hold when the pestle was raised ready for the stroke. Broken pestles were sometimes pecked into new and shorter ones. Some pestles were painted. Some were so long that they would quickly become shattered by actual use" (Hudson & Blackburn 1983:121).

Other stone implements included the stone anvil, a small round rock with a slight divot where the acorn was placed before striking. The hammer was in turn a small round hand held rock. Metates were stone slabs where seeds were ground up by the hand held mano. Metates and manos predate the mortar and pestle by many thousands of years with the latter replacing them several thousand years ago. The Chumash also had curious round stones with holes in the center shaped vaguely like a donut. These have proven to be weights for digging sticks although they may also have been used for war clubs and fishing weights. Some of these objects are polished and decorated with designs incised into the stone and may have been used in for ritual purposes such as the head of a sunstaff used in the winter solstice ceremonies.

Comals, introduced by the Spanish during mission times were flat, rectangular, slightly concave stones with a hole at one end so they could be taken from the fire with a hooked stick. They were used like frying pans. A similar object was used by the Indians in prehistoric times for heating liquid in a basket.

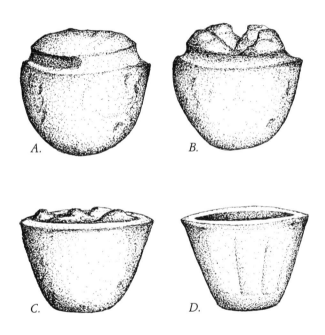

The four steps to making a mortar.
A. A suitable round piece of sandstone is
selected. A stone chisel and hand held hammer
stone are used to peck a groove around the top
edge of the mortar. B. Knobs of sandstone are
pecked in the top and then lopped off with a
strong blow. C. The rim is formed and the
final contour of the outer edge is started.
D. To finish, the bowl of the mortar is pecked
out (Bryan 1961).

Small stone pestle. Author's collection.

Grey sandstone pestle from Shell Beach area.
Courtesy Bruce and Patricia Miller.

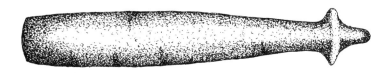

*Pestle. Typical of the Chumash golden age in
the mainland coast area.*

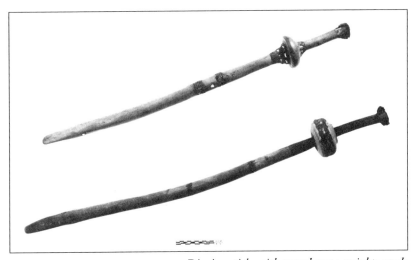

*Digging sticks with round stone weights made
for Henry Henshaw by Juan Pico in 1894.
Courtesy of the Smithsonian Institution.*

Steatite cooking bowl. Height: 13 inches.
Courtesy of the San Luis Obispo County
Historical Museum.

Comal. Steatite frying pan introduced by the
Spanish. This example is unusual in that it has
four holes for the poker stick that retrieves it
from the fire rather than one as is common.
Courtesy of the Ventura County
Historical Museum.

Steatite bowl inlaid with shell beads.
Photograph courtesy of Museum of the
American Indian, Heye Foundation.

Steatite pipe with bird bone stem.

MATERIAL CULTURE

STEATITE EFFIGIES

CHUMASH EFFIGIES ARE largely zoomorphic in form consisting mainly of marine mammals and water birds although canoes and pendants were also made. They were used as a kind of personal talisman or erected as shrines. They were made of stone, mainly steatite because of its relatively soft nature and its ability to take a good finish. Sandstone serpentine, wood and bone were also used in some areas.

Effigies made from steatite often have a high black gloss probably obtained by first greasing and then smoking the surface before polishing. These effigies have both a ritual and economic significance for the Chumash with particular effigies possibly having a specific meaning. Pelican effigy stones are thought to have been fishing talismans and owl effigies may have been used by shamans for curing.

The Chumash were fond of making steatite killer whales, an animal which they regarded favorably because it supposedly herded seals ashore for slaughter.

They also had an extensive range of other animals which they choose to represent in steatite, among them, the California grey whale, sea otter, California sea lion, herons, pelicans, and seals. There is a single representation of a raven extant, a bird that was significant in Chumash mythology. It should be noted that there is some question as to the authenticity of these particular "realistic" effigies. Some consider them to be latter day fakes.

Chumash effigies can be divided into two rough stylistic categories for identification purposes: realistic and abstract. The realistic figurines often have natural attributes, such as drilled eyes, blowholes, mouth incisions, and dorsal fins. Commonly effigies have decorative incising or shell bead inlay (Hoover 1974:34).

A large group of pelican stones found by de Cessac in 1877-1879 on San Nicolas Island are primarily abstract representations and have no incising or bead inlay. Some of them have carved bird-like markings that represent wings or other avian anatomy.

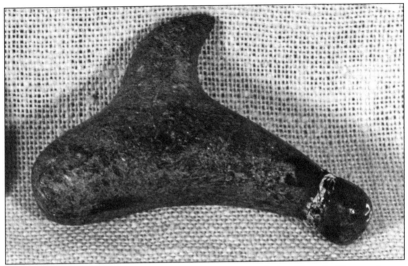

*Steatite whale effigy. A fiber cord once
wrapped the tail of this killer whale talisman.
Whale effigies were called caxnipaxat by the
Chumash. Courtesy of the Ventura County
Historical Museum (Hudson & Blackburn
1986:171).*

Canoe effigies were used by the canoe makers and fisherman as a sort of dream charm. Fernando Librado, a Harrington consultant provided this information.

> "These little boats serve as a charm so that he will always have luck in fishing. The baby boats are not any good to anyone else. When a person wants to be a good fisherman he drinks *toloache* and has a dream. He dreams about canoes and sees himself out at sea becoming a good fisherman, for a spirit or something shows him the future. A canoe charm dreamer need not be a canoe owner, however, any more than a whale dreamer is the owner of a whale.
>
> When a canoe charm dreamer dies, these effigy canoes — sometimes several — are buried with him. Many of the tiny boats have been found in graves of the ancient people at various places. Such graves must have been those of canoemakers. The little boats which are found in such a grave are no longer of value, for their owner is dead, and it was he who knew how to manipulate the charms" (Hudson, Timbrook and Rempe 1978:126).

Steatite seal effigy attributed to the Chumash.
San Nicolas Island. Courtesy of the Catalina
Island Museum.

Steatite dog effigy attributed to the Chumash
with shell bead inlay eyes. San Nicolas Island.
Courtesy of the Catalina Island Museum.

Steatite killer whale effigy attributed to the
Chumash. San Nicolas Island. Courtesy of the
Catalina Island Museum.

MATERIAL CULTURE

HUNTING

OF ALL THE activities in which the Chumash excelled it was the securing of food where they were eminently practical and being such they developed a technology consistent with their needs. They did not farm or make use of even basic agriculture methods until the Spanish came. But they were marvelous hunters and that added to the their highly developed gathering activity, gave them a large subsistence base.

For hunting they used bows and arrows, javelins, curved throwing sticks, clubs, slings, various types of snares, deadfall and box traps, decoys and all the wiles of a people close to nature. They were by all accounts very proficient hunters and expert marksmen.

Two types of bow were used, the self bow for small game and the sinew backed bow for fighting and for larger animals such as deer. The self bow is an unadorned staff of wood about three and a half to four and half feet in length. They were fashioned out of elderberry, juniper, and nascent oak. Self bows were kept unstrung until they were ready to shoot and were much liked because they could be strung while running. Bowstring was made of two or three ply woven vegetable fiber (red milkweed) or deer sinew.

Sinew backed bows were under four feet in length, and made of toyon and elder and have pin type nocks. The best sinew backed bows were bent with the use of hot water, unlike lesser bows that were shaped by placing the bow staff in fire. The sinew backed bow was curved and then recurved at the tip ends. To attach the sinew, pitch was smeared evenly on the bow staff and then the sinew was laid on in strips, then more sinew was wrapped radially to greatly increase the strength of the wood. Bows and arrows were often painted red with iron oxide. A Harrington informant said that arrows painted red would not work on birds because the bird would see the red color like its own image in a mirror and fly away (Hudson & Blackburn 1982).

Various types of arrows have been documented as being used by the Chumash. The self arrow was a shaft of straightened wood with feather fletch-

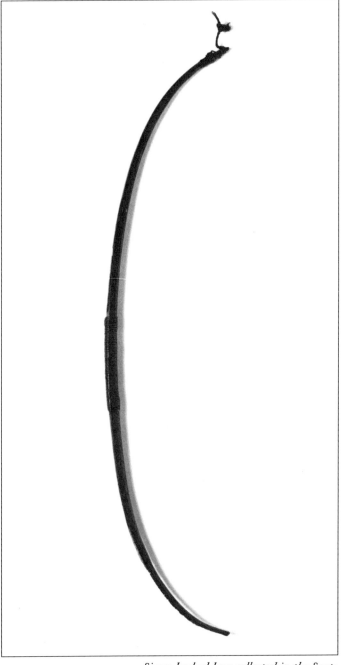

*Sinew-backed bow collected in the Santa
Barbara area by Vancouver in 1793. Courtesy of
the British Museum.*

ing, V shaped notchs and fire hardened points. These arrows were made of toyon and were used for hunting small game or for sporting competition.

Composite arrows were the most elaborate and longest of the arrows the Chumash used. With sinew wrapping, radial fletchings, and painted or pyrographic decorations, these arrows were things of a terrible beauty, deadly and wonderful in the making. Carrizo cane was cut and allowed to dry completely, then straighten by a heated, grooved straightening stone. When straight, a firesharpened hardwood shaft was attached with sinew to one end by inserting it into the hollow cane and then wrapping the sinew radially. On the other end a hardwood nock was inserted and then attached with sinew. On a stone tipped cane arrow, a chert point would be attached to the hardwood foreshaft before it was inserted into the cane mainshaft. Hafting the chert point to the hardwood shaft was done with asphaltum cement and very fine sinew. Fletching was attached with sinew wrapping and trimmed with a hot coal to the desired shape (Hudson 1974).

Chumash arrow points were most often chert although imported obsidian was also used. They were made by pressure flaking rather than percussion and were triangular or laurel leaf shaped with tangs. Many had notched and rounded bases.

The Chumash hunters used decoy headdresses to approach their prey without startling it. Deer and antelope headdresses were commonly used to good advantage. Costansó with the Portolá expedition in 1769 commented:

Deadfall trap. A large rock is canted over another with the aid of a short stick. The stick and an acorn as bait are the trigger which when tripped crushes any animal unlucky enough to be underneath (Hudson & Blackburn 1982:59).

"In killing deer and antelopes, they employ an admirable device. They preserve the skin of the head and part of the neck of one of these animals...This mask they put like a cap on the head. On seeing a deer or antelope, they crawl slowly with the left hand on the ground, carrying the bow and four arrows in the right. They lower and raise the head, turning it from one side to the other, and make other movements so characteristic of these animals, that they attract them without difficulty to the decoy, and having them at short range, they discharge their arrows with sure effect" (Hemert-Engert and Teggart 1910:49).

It is believed that the Chumash used arrow poisons, certainly the Gabrielinos to the south used them but the efficacy of these organic poisons has not been determined. Slings were also used for killing birds and small game. Seals and sea lions were hunted with clubs and spears. The Indians would wait until the seals were ashore and then get between them and the water, trapping the beasts. In the struggle to get back to sea a few would be bludgeoned.

Hunting was a rewarding activity for the Chumash. Game was plentiful and not overly difficult to catch so that winter proved to be the only time when food was scarce.

Stone tipped composite arrow. A chert point is lashed to the wooden foreshaft with sinew and asphaltum.

Wooden tipped composite arrow.

Steatite arrow straightener. 3 inches. Courtesy of Mission San Luis Obispo Museum.

Double grooved arrow straightening stone. A cane arrowshaft was straightened by placing it in the groove of the heated steatite stone and then applying the correct pressure as it cooled. Courtesy of Mission San Luis Obispo Museum.

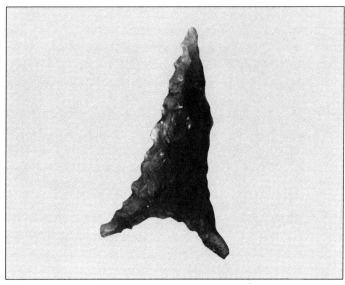

Chalcedony point. Length 1 inch. Excavated at the China Town dig in San Luis Obispo, 1987. Courtesy of the San Luis Obispo County Historical Museum.

FISHING
CANOES

FISH AND SHELLFISH in lesser amounts, were a mainstay in the Chumash diet. But fish are not easily taken from the ocean even when you have the ability go to sea. So the Chumash had to become great and ingenious fishermen to harvest this bounty and they did just that with admirable skill. Their fishing gear and canoes are remarkable in design and eminently practical in use.

To travel on water the Chumash built three types of canoes, the plank canoe, the dugout and the tule balsa canoe. The plank canoe they called *Tomol*. For fishing gear they had harpoons, fishspears, hook, line and sinker, fish nets, bone gorges and dip nets. With this gear and their sea going craft they sought what the sea had to offer — fish, seals, sea otters, shark and even sea birds. They fished throughout the year taking advantage of the relatively calm seas of the Channel, and the annual runs of albacore, yellow and blue fin tuna and some of the smaller pelagic fishes such as sardines which the larger tunas preyed upon.

Their fishing was heavier in the summer months when these fish were running. In the winter months they relied more on easily obtained shellfish (some of the best low tides occur in winter) or dried fish caught in the fair weather months. It is likely that some of the large coastal population moved inland seasonally thus reducing the subsistence needs in the coast villages.

What freshwater fishing was done was minimal and done when the opportunity presented itself, like the catching of steelhead during the annual run. Such anadromous fish were readily caught by fishspears, and weir nets in dammed up pools.

CANOES

The planked canoe of the Chumash was unique in North America and it was this canoe which allowed them to travel to the islands and to fish the

Aquatic design elements in a Chumash rock painting (SBa 1380, Cave C.), (Hudson & Conti 1984).

Tomol, The Chumash plank canoe.

abundant schools of pelagic fish that visited the Santa Barbara Channel. It was their finest technological achievement impressing all the early explorers who saw the canoes in use. Font gave an excellent description of the *tomol*.

"They are very carefully made of several planks which they work with no other tools but their shells and flints. They join them at the seams by sewing them with very strong thread which they have and fit the joints with pitch...Some of the launches are decorated with little shells and all are painted red with hematite. In shape they are like a little boat without ribs, ending in two points...In the middle there is a somewhat elevated plank laid across from side to side to serve as a seat and to preserve the convexity of the frame. Each launch is composed of some twenty long and narrow pieces...They carry some poles about six feet in length which end in blades, these being the oars with which they row alternately on one side and then on the other" (Bolton 1930:252).

Much of what is known about Chumash watercraft is due to Fernando Librado, a Chumash informant and to the diligence of John P. Harrington in taking his information down. In 1978, Hudson, Timbrook, and Rempe edited *Tomol: Chumash Watercraft as Described in the Ethnographic Notes of John P. Harrington*. This is a prime source for information on Chumash canoes and was used in part for the following account.

Fernando Librado was an utterly remarkable man. A Ventureño Chumash who lived to the age of 76 and who could remember stories he had been told about Mission times. He related this account of the plank canoe to John Harrington.

> "The board canoe was the house of the sea. It was more valuable than a land house and was worth much money...Only the canoe makers know how to build a canoe. They are called *'altomolich*, meaning "maker of canoes," for they have learned how to do it under older men. They are the ones who know how, and only they for no one else was allowed to hang around. Only certain men in a village knew how. An old canoemaker would have his helpers and he would allow no one else around. There was much to know. Then the boards had to be fitted together well. The boards had to be tarred and tied. They used no iron in building a board canoe. They knew all the secrets in order to make a *tomol* which was agile on the sea...With their tools the Indians were united in spirit. They had plenty of time to take in their canoe workmanship. The old-time people had good eyes, and they would just look at a thing and see if it was right. No one hurried them up—it was not like the Whites. The Indians wanted to build good canoes and they did not care how long it would take. A long time was needed if they were going to make a good canoe...Sometimes the Indians would finish building a canoe in about forty days, but sometimes it took from two to six months before it was done" (Hudson, Timbrook & Rempe 1978:39-41).

The use of the plank canoe was not widespread. Only two California tribes had it, the Chumash and the Gabrielinos to the south, who probably obtained the technology from the Chumash. It is thought that the *tomol* was of local origin even so the upper parts of the Chumash realm did not have the plank canoe until Mission times.

The early balsa boats and dugout canoes of Chumash origin were not ideal for extensive maritime navigation. Elsewhere dugouts were quite seaworthy but in Chumash territory there were no suitable tree species for large seagoing dugouts, consequently the Chumash developed an alternate technology. It is thought that around 500 A. D. the Chumash, in an effort to make their dugouts more seaworthy, might have added some hull planks around the top edge of their dugouts. Eventually more hull planks were added and the dugout sides were reduced to a large bottom plank. Archaeological evidence such as canoe caulking, plugs, drills and the additional evidence of a full blown maritime economy in the Channel area at this time suggests that a seagoing canoe was in use.

The plank canoe was frameless, with no internal structural ribs and was made from driftwood, mainly redwood or from pine that grew in the Santa Barbara and Ventura back country. Redwood from the north would float down the coast after a storm and land on the Channel beaches. There it was collected and brought to the villages to dry. Redwood is relatively light and has the essential qualities of being easily worked as well as durable.

Wood for canoe making was very carefully selected with a straight grain and no knots. Knots would dry out and crack causing the boat to leak. The best wood available was used for the bottom plank and the first row around the hull. Larger pieces of wood were split with a whale bone wedge or deer antler and then shaped, trimmed and leveled with adzes and a chert knife. The usual adze had a blade made from a sharpened Pismo clam shell. After the planks were split those selected for hull boards were beveled and finished with sharkskin sandpaper.

Canoe paddle blade collected by Vancouver in 1793. Note the repair made with fiber cord and asphaltum. Courtesy of the British Museum.

Malak was what the Chumash called hard tar which when mixed with ground pine pitch in a stone jar and boiled would form *yop*. With this mixture they caulked each row of planks that made the hull of the *tomol*.

Holes were bored in the hull planks using hand drills tipped with chert or bone. The planks were then laid edge to edge and lashed together with *tok* — red milkweed fiber string. The *tok* was double and triple-wrapped to give the hull additional strength. Once fitted and lashed, caulking tule, which was the heart of dry tule rush was forced into the cracks on the outside of the canoe hull. The hull was then coated with *yop* again.

Next a structural crossplank was added at midship to reinforce the craft. This was never used as a seat. Finally, splashboards were attached to the gunwales, stern and prow. These semi-circles had both an ornamental purpose as well as the immediately practical function of keeping the surf out.

With the structural elements complete the *tomol* was sanded and painted. The red ochre paint acted as a sealant that greatly enhanced the integrity of the boat. Shell inlay was added for decoration to the outside in traditional geometric designs.

Tomols were both fast and light and varied in length from ten to thirty feet although occasionally they were as small as eight feet. The plank canoe was propelled with a double bladed paddle. There was no anchor although the canoe was sometimes held in place while at sea by pulling kelp over the side to keep it from drifting. Otherwise the fisherman would just drift with the current as they fished.

Only men used and made the *tomol* and they belonged to the Brotherhood of the Canoe, one of the Chumash craft guilds. They called each other "relatives" and all others non-relatives. The main activities of the Brotherhood were to build canoes, to fish, and to keep up the sea going trade with the Channel Islands. They were guardians of the traditions of the canoe and some of the most powerful men in Chumash society (Hudson, Timbrook and Rempe 1978).

The tule balsa canoe was used by the Chumash in lagoons and at sea. It was quickly built: start to finish from the cutting of the tule to the launching of the boat would take as little as three days.

To make the tule canoe, green bulrush (*Scirpus acutus*) was cut and then spread out to dry. After a few days when the tule was partially dried it was taken up and formed into bundles, the length of which depended on the size of the boat to be made. The bundle that formed the bottom of the canoe was much larger than the others. A willow pole ran the length of each bundle to add strength to the body of the canoe. Bundles were tied together at the stern and prow to form a raised point and then tied to the bottom bundle along their length. There was no seat in the balsa canoe. Finally, the outside of the canoe was coated with tar to add buoyancy and prevent rot (Hudson, Timbrook, Rempe 1978:27-31).

The tule canoe was bulky but lightweight and easily carried overhead. When cared for properly these canoes were both versatile and durable. It is said that the Chumash could even make a fire on board these craft to attract and cook fish. They did this by coating the interior section of the canoe with a hardened mud on which the fire was started. Water was always handy so there was little chance of a fire getting out of control.

Tule canoes were also furnished with a double bladed paddle for propulsion or were paddled with the arms when lying in the prone position. They were mainly used for near-shore fishing in natural harbors and bays but occasionally trips to the Islands were made.

There is very little known about the dugout canoe that the Chumash used. There are no known examples of this type of craft surviving, and very few historical accounts mention it. The dugout was propelled with paddle or long willow pole and used mainly for fishing in estuaries and calm water. It is about twenty to thirty feet in length and made of a solid tree trunk probably willow although cottonwood may have been used (Hudson & Blackburn 1982:338).

MATERIAL CULTURE

THE CHUMASH USED a great variety of fishing tackle. Consummate fisherman, they developed and used all the standard methods of gathering from sea and stream. Lobster traps and crab nets were conical and made of willow sticks. The lobster would enter at one end and then be caught within the wicker structure. Dip nets were used for catching sardines. They were about three feet in diameter, very deep and could be closed with a drawstring. Pedro Fages, a lieutenant with the Portolá expedition, commented on this type of net.

> "For catching sardines, they use large baskets, into which they throw the bait which these fish like, which is ground up leaves of cactus, so that they come in great numbers. The Indians then make their cast and catch great numbers of sardines" (Priestley 1937:51).

Drag nets, seine nets, and gill nets were all used. Netting was knotted fiber made from sea grass or milkweed fiber. Both men and women worked on cordage and the Chumash spent a lot of time making and repairing these nets. Fishing, though, was primarily a male activity.

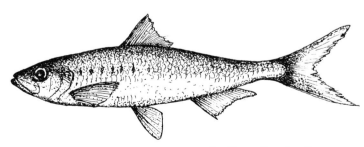

Pacific sardine, Sardinops sagax.

The seine net was used much the same way a gill net operates except that it had wooden floats suspending the net in the water as well as large stone sinkers to keep it vertical. The nets were large, and deployed in a circular fashion from a canoe. The net enclosure then snagged any fish that happened by and were especially effective for large fish whose gills were caught in the netting.

In freshwater streams, stone weirs were made and weir traps made of willow sticks formed in a conical fashion were placed at an opening in the artificial dam. The Indians then went upstream and scared the fish into the trap. Sometimes soap plant (*Chlorogalum pomeridianum*) was used to drug trout to the point where they would float to the surface of a stream.

The Chumash fished in the sea and at the surf line with hook, line and sinker. Hooks were made of bent cactus spines, shell, wood and bone. The circular fish hook was common and usually made from abalone shell, with bone and mussel shell used to a lesser extent. Common bait for fishing was cactus, black mussel, and clams (Hoover 1973). Bone gorges are the simplest of all hooks, merely a straight bipointed piece of bone that is attached at the center to a line. The hook is dangled in the water until a fish is attracted and takes a bite. A quick jerk lodges the unbaited hook crossways in the fish's mouth.

The Chumash also used tridents and simple fish spears with bone or wooden points, and harpoon arrows with detachable points that could be reeled in once the fish was speared. Harpoons were about six feet long with barbed points and detachable foreshafts. Harpoons had a single barb and a chert point. Line was attached to the foreshaft and when the harpoon was thrown, a few coils were held in the throwing hand to be loosed when the spear was in flight. They were used for hunting large fish and sea otters. There is not much evidence that the Chumash hunted whales with these harpoons although they did readily eat whale when it washed ashore (Hudson & Blackburn 1982:149-225).

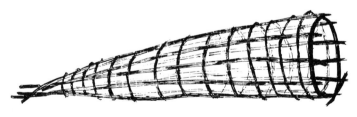

Conical wicker fish trap. After being submerged in place at the opening in a fish weir, fish were driven down the creek into the trap (Hudson & Blackburn 1982:149).

*(A.) Circular bone fish hook. (B.) Circular shell
fish hook made from the shoulder of an
abalone shell.*

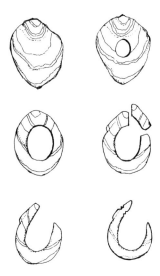

*How a circular shell fishhook is made.
A circular piece of shell, usually haliotis, is
broken off with a hammerstone. A chert drill
with the aid of an abrasive sand and water
paste perforates the round piece of shell. The
hole is widened by grinding and the outside is
smoothed and rounded by rubbing on a stone
slab. The tip of the hook and the shank are
separated by removing a piece of shell and or
further grinding. The point of the circular shell
hook is smoothed and sharpened and notches
are made in the shank to hold the fiber string.*

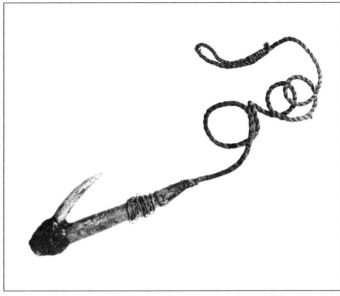

Composite fishhook with bone point attached to wooden shank by fiber twine and asphaltum. Courtesy of the British Museum.

Harpoon collected by Vancouver in 1793. Courtesy of the British Museum.

Harpoon foreshaft collected by Vancouver in 1793. Courtesy of the British Museum.

MATERIAL CULTURE

Food

THE CHUMASH DID not practice primitive agriculture as did the tribes along the Colorado River. There is historical mention of them scattering seeds in cleared areas around their villages although this was probably a religious exercise. They also kept dogs and fattened the occasional bear cub but otherwise they had no domestic animals; cattle, sheep and pigs were all introduced by the Spanish. They gathered a wide range of wild foods, fished the streams and ocean and hunted native game. Their diet was broadly based and included virtually every good source of protein and nutrition in their area. However, two sources of food were of paramount importance to the Chumash. These were fish and acorns.

Fish was eaten in all manner of ways, dried, raw, skewered, roasted and wrapped in leaves and baked in an earth oven. Historical evidence suggests that the Chumash preferred the fish roasted over other ways of cooking. Over 150 types of fish remains including great white shark, mako shark, and most of the pelagic tuna have been found in Chumash kitchen middens.

Acorns were prepared by removing the outer shell. The acorn cap was discarded and the nut was placed on a flat stone and then tapped with any handy oval stone or mano. The nut meats were then placed in raised, storage basket granaries to dry. To eat, the cured nuts were crushed in a mortar until they were rough flour. This acorn meal was then placed in a shallow pit lined with grass or leaves and leached repeatedly by pouring hot water over it until the bitter tannin was washed away. The Chumash, being fine basket makers, no doubt used leaching baskets when they were available. Once leached, the acorn meal could be stored for later use. Acorn gruel was cooked by dropping red hot stones in a watertight basket that had been filled with acorn flour and water. A less common way of eating acorn meal was to form it into flat cakes to be cooked on a steatite *comal* at the edge of the campfire.

Seasonality was another factor in Chumash food gathering. In the fall the village activity would center around acorn gathering. Large amounts of acorns

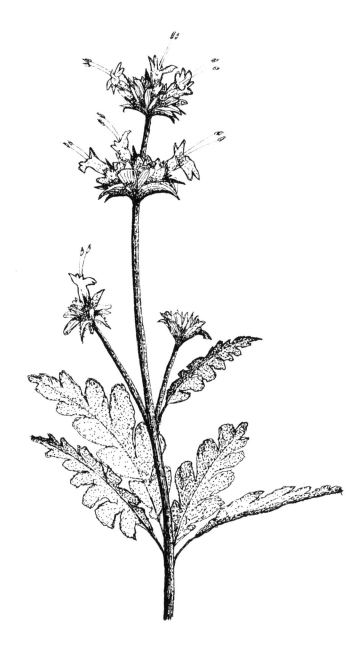

Chia sage, Salvia Columbariae. Common in dry open places below 5000 feet. The seed was roasted for food and used for a refreshing drink.

were gathered and stored in basket granaries. Whole huts were set aside as storage places for the massive quantities of nuts collected. One full-bearing California Live Oak might drop as many as several hundred pounds of acorn nuts.

The population size of villages would change depending on the time of year and the food gathering needs. During the few best weeks when the oaks dropped their acorns a large effort would be made to gather as much as possible before moisture or the rodent and avian competition reduced the yield. Temporary gathering camps might have been used thus drawing much of a village population inland from the coast.

In the summer and fall the Channel fishing was at its height. In the spring, cresses and new shoots were gathered for eating. Winter was called "the time when people get hungry," in the Spanish *interrogatorios* (Landberg 1965:96).

The geography of the Chumash territory dictated the types of food that were abundant in a particular area. The Coastal Chumash living near the Channel within its Mediterranean climate or living on the slightly colder northern shoreline were more heavily dependent on fish and marine animals. The Inland Chumash, gaining a living in the arid back country or high coniferous forests, relied more on acorns and deer for their sustenance.

Many types of seeds, fruits and berries were eaten, among them: blackberry, elderberry, hollyleaf cherry, strawberries, prickly pear, rose fruit, pine nuts, chia sage, grass seeds, and seeds of various wildflowers. Tubers, bulbs, (brodiaea, mariposa lily) roots, mushrooms, tree fungi, madrone, yucca, and seaweed also added variety to the Chumash diet.

The Indians had an ingenious way of obtaining sugar. Honeydew is the sweet droppings from insects such as aphids and whiteflies left as a thin residue on carrizo grass in the summer months. The grass stems were cut down and threshed in great numbers. The crystallized excreta was then collected from the winnowing basket or flat tule mat and made into sticky balls. This "sugar" was then eaten as a dessert and said to be the color of brown sugar. A sweet drink was made from crushed manzanita berries and cold water. Honey was obtained in small quantities from wild bees. Bee larvae as well as yellow jacket and hornet larvae were also eaten as delicacies (Orr 1956).

Soap plant was used by the Chumash in a variety of ways, as a fish poison, as soap in the sweat lodges and as food. Its bulb was dug up, cleaned and roasted. The tender stalk of young yucca plant was eaten in a similar fashion or placed in the ground with hot cooking stones covered over with earth and left over night and then eaten for breakfast.

In 1942, Harrington published a checklist of animals eaten. Also consult Landberg, *The Chumash Indians of Southern California* (1965) which gives a great deal of information on specific food items.

MATERIAL CULTURE

CLOTHING

IT IS CLEAR that the Chumash wore few clothes and living in a relatively mild climate, clothing was not an absolute necessity. Numerous early references describe them as going about virtually naked. No doubt there were times in the winter when clothing was needed. Festivals and ritual ceremonies also presented an opportunity to wear finery.

The historical record gives us some idea of how the Chumash dressed and what functions they attributed to clothing. The Spanish outsiders for one reason or another — seasonality, scant knowledge of Chumash social hierarchy or even faulty reporting present a confusing picture. Although early reports of Chumash clothing suggest that it was worn for protection from the elements and for warmth and not for reasons of modesty or social standing, it is clear with the additional ethnographic reporting from J.P. Harrington and a careful review of the historical record that clothing did indeed have social significance and played an important role in defining Chumash self image. Richer and more powerful people in the village, the chiefs, crafts specialists and the canoe owners dressed in more "expensive" apparel, including bear and otter fur. The poor people had less and their clothing showed it. They wore more "common" materials, grass and shredded tree bark. Clothing, even as it does in our own day, was representative of a classed society.

Chumash women particularly of the lower class wore woven tule or grass skirts. Sometimes these plant fiber skirts were made the bark of willow, cottonwood or sycamore trees. The inner bark was cut from the tree in strips and shredded into fibers, then interwoven with fiber string to make a serviceable skirt. When tule or sea grass was used small globular pieces of asphaltum were pinched on to the bottom end of the tule to weight it down so as to keep the skirt hanging correctly in the wind. The women also wore tanned and worked deerskin in the manner of a skirt, wrapping it around their waist and hanging a variety of shells on the fringe for decoration (Hudson & Blackburn 1985:27-40).

Generally men wore nothing except a belt that was really a bit of netting or a fiber string from which they could suspend tools and food. Hide capes were worn in cold weather and were sewn skins, usually deer, rabbit, sea otter and bear. They were worn by both men and women and often had a pin-shaped shell or bone fastener permanently sewn onto one side. It was a sleeveless garment worn over the neck and shoulders and reaching either to the small of the back or as far down as the ankles in the usual manner of a cape. It is probable that capes were worn by the elite and signified a social standing, perhaps that of a chief or canoe owner. Social standing may also have been indicated by the type of animal skin worn although they seemed to have used a wide range (Hudson & Blackburn 1985:52).

Men, especially members of the ruling elite, wore on ritual occasions a net skirt woven from fiber cordage and hemmed with hanging feathers. A more elaborate down cord skirt was also worn. Here, down feathers were interwoven

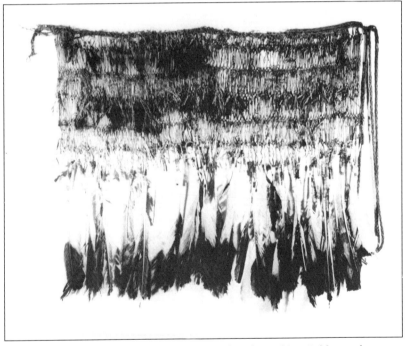

Feathered net skirt. Golden eagle & crow feathers are tied to fiber cord net with sinew. This ritual garment was worn around the waist during the performance of a number of Chumash dances. Courtesy Southwest Museum.

or twisted on fiber strands that hung from a belt. The hem was a fringe of tail and wing feathers. This ceremonial skirt was only for ritual use and not worn as a daily occurrence.

Headgear for protection from the sun and for cushioning when carrying burdens was a basket cap made of coiled juncus decorated with traditional designs. Men also wore a finely made hair net decorated with shell bead money and probably fashioned from milkweed fiber.

Ritual headgear for dances displayed some of the most beautiful and impressive craftwork of the Chumash. They set their imaginations to work on these ceremonial costumes making fiber-net robes and skirts with feathers attached and headbands decorated with small shell beads on a base of deerskin. Feather headbands were made from hundreds of bright orange vertically arranged quills of the red-shafted flicker and worn in rainmaking rituals. Headbands were probably worn with other ritual paraphernalia like feathered skirts and robes creating a wonderful and mysterious effect.

The topknot headdress and others used in specific ceremonial dances were loaded with plumage and were marvelous examples of the spiritual manifested in the real. Favorite feathers were eagle, magpie, or owl depending on the dance (Hudson & Blackburn 1985:159-203).

Bear costumes were intricately made, having reins for manipulation and hollow gourds attached within for sound effects. A man enrobed in this outfit could swagger about in a malevolent fashion and be quite impressive when viewed from afar. It was made from the skin of a black bear and worn by a special "bear doctor." It was kept in a secret place, a cave perhaps, and many people believed that a shaman could physically turn himself into a bear. This bear ritual was part power dance meant for sacred purposes and was performed both in the open and in secret (Hudson & Blackburn 1985:154-158).

The Chumash preferred to go barefoot although they did occasionally take recourse in hide sandals or sandals made from yucca fiber or soft tree bark. The hide sandal was cut in the shape of a foot from the thickest parts of deerskin near the neck or tail and had straps that wrapped around the top of the foot and ankle.

Shell bead necklaces were a favorite type of ornamentation. Strands of shell beads were often worn in great numbers. The bead types were red and black abalone, clam and olivella shells. Stone and seed beads were also combined with shell beads as spacers and for a variation in design. These bead necklaces were worn around the head or the neck and represented wealth. Earrings and bracelets consisted of bone, wood and shell. Rod like pieces of dark wood, mainly elderberry were worn in pierced ear lobes. Bone and shell nose rods were also worn in a pierced nasal septum. Some nose rods and earrings were the whitish columella shell decorated with a dark spiral of asphaltum.

*Stone bead necklace from San Luis Obispo area
collected by James Terry in 1875. Photograph
by Travis Hudson, courtesy of the American
Museum of Natural History.*

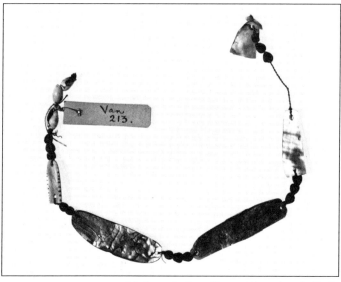

*Abalone shell necklace with seed and olivella
shell spacers. Vancouver 1793. Courtesy of the
British Museum.*

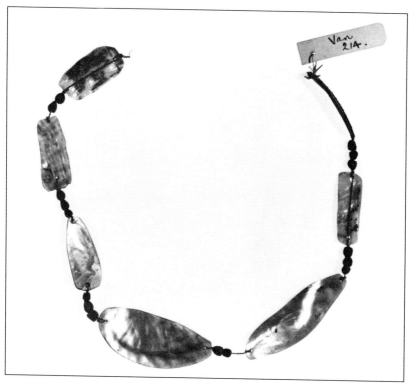

Abalone shell necklace strung on fiber twine.
Vancouver 1793. Courtesy of the
British Museum.

Shell nose rod. Polished tubular shell with
asphaltum filled spiral groove. Worn in a hole
in the nasal septum.

Abalone shell bead necklace with discs resembling buttons. Strung with hide and fiber. Vancouver 1793. Courtesy of the British Museum.

Other accessories were purses and tobacco bags from hide as well as tubes made from carrizo cane or elderberry wood often filled with tobacco or medicine. Combs were made from bone and shell and brushes from soaproot fiber and asphaltum. Striking incised hairpins made from bone or wood were used by men to keep their hair in place which was generally coiled with the spatulate hairpin stuck vertically through the coil across the back of the head. The pins range in size from a few inches to a foot and a half and many of the bone examples have a perforation at the top end. They were worn in daily life as well as being used to attach ritual headdresses during the execution of ceremonial dances.

They also made great use of body paints, usually red or black and red mixed to a sooty brown. Body paints were both decorative and functional. They could denote social status or station for example the Chief's messenger would paint his face with white over black in imitation of the markings on a mudhen. Women would cover their bodies with a red ochre to prevent sunburn and giving their upper bodies a glossy look. Face painting in stripes, checkers and zigzags was common during celebrations (Hudson & Blackburn 1985:316).

So even in their apparent nakedness as was so often described by early visitors there was an abundance of clothing possibilities for the Chumash.

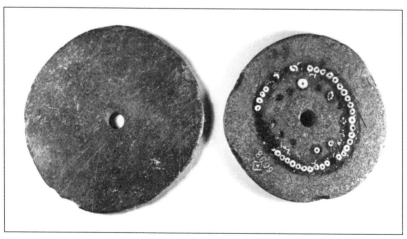

Steatite disk shirt ornaments, one with shell bead overlay. Photograph by Travis Hudson, courtesy of the American Museum of Natural History.

*Bone Hairpins with shell bead inlay. One
specimen is topped off with an abalone pearl.
Photograph courtesy of the Museum of the
American Indian, Heye Foundation.*

*Feathered cane hairpin collected by Vancouver
in 1793. In this specimen bark and fiber string
is wrapped around a piece of yellow cane.
Strings of black and white shell beads make an
ornamental base for some clipped black
feathers. 21 cm. Courtesy of the
British Museum.*

SHELTER

THE CHUMASH LIVED in tule thatched houses that were hemispherical or conical in shape. Several early Spanish explorers described them as having the shape of half oranges with an open smokehole for ventilation and light at the top near the center. These circular huts were from 15 feet to 50 feet in diameter and could house as few as one family or as many as 50 people. They were surprisingly large and roomy when you went indoors.

Houses were carefully made of tule thatch and arched wooden poles. The housing site within the village was orderly, laid out in rows or in a spaced but random pattern with trails leading between each hut. They were probably spaced close enough to be convenient but far enough away so as not to catch fire from one to the other. Some houses had several tule mats hung in the doorway, one on the inside that moved inward and one on the outside to form a double screen against the wind.

This type of house was quickly and easily built and quite sound, able to keep even the coldest winter at bay. Tule thatch up to a half a foot thick was excellent insulation. In short, it was quite serviceable and in time when damage became great either by insect pests or weather it could easily be torched and a new clean domicile built.

When the Chumash set out to build a house, one man would first lay out a true circle by holding a pole upright at the center of the housing site. A fiber string was tied to the top of this pole. A pointed stick used for inscribing the ground was tied to the other end of the string. The man would then pull the fiber string taut and walk in a circular fashion using this primitive compass to mark the ground with the sharp end of the stick. After tracing a circle on the house site, holes for the willow structural poles were dug about two feet apart with digging sticks and shell scoops. The long willow poles, which were both pliable and strong, were then placed into the holes the tapering ends pointing skyward. The tops of these poles were then brought together in an overlapping fashion and tied with fiber string or willow bark to their opposite

Unfinished tule thatched hut showing willow framework. Whale jaw bones were sometimes used to bar the door.

number forming the vertical ribs and ceiling of the house. Some houses had one or two poles which were allowed to extend beyond the top of the smokehole. Here the owner of the house could later tie a hide mat when it rained. The poles which formed the structural elements of the house were 15 to 25 feet tall. On the Islands where trees and thatching materials were scarce some of the structural elements were made from whale bones or manzanita branches. In all likelyhood these houses were smaller than those on the mainland.

The floor was bare dirt or sometimes a fine clean beach sand was spread on it. The earth floor was hardened by water and pounding to form a surface that could be kept relatively clean.

The horizontal elements of the house structure were more long willow poles but thinner this time. Once in place, thatch was then folded over the horizontals in an overlapping fashion so that they were not visible. Thatch was carrizo cane, tule, bracken fern, cattail and on the islands, sea grass was used. If tule or carrizo cane was used the first layer of thatch was started on the bottom of the pole infrastructure. The tule stalks were placed butt end into the ground and tip end up, dirt was then heaped up around the base of the outer wall to keep rodents out. On all subsequent layers the thatch was placed with the tip ends on the outer surface and pointed down as common sense and weather proofing would demand (Hudson & Blackburn 1983: 325).

The door was positioned east or west to catch the morning or evening sunlight. Many doors were framed with whale bones and or tied bundles of tule. Some houses even had small "windows". The fire pit was in the center of the hut in a shallow declivity in the dirt floor below the smokehole. The area around the fire was surrounded by flat stones.

Inside the thatched house, tule mats were used as room partitions and mattresses. Furnishing included stools and tables from wood or whale vertebrae. Beds were raised platforms four or five feet above the floor with a mattress of loose tule, straw, or reed matting. Blankets were sewn furs, especially bearskins, sea grass, and loosely woven cotton which they obtained from the tribes to the east, primarily the Mohave Indians (Hudson & Blackburn 1983:323-439).

The sweathouse was another structure found in a typical Chumash village. The Spanish called them *temescales*. The *temescal* was used daily by the Chumash men. It was an activity which they clearly relished for its rejuvenating effects. Made of woven boughs and coated with mud these sweathouses served a number of purposes.

The large *temescal* was dome shaped, held many people and was used for both ritual and secular activities. In the middle of the semi-subterranean lodge a fire is built directly under an opening which serves as a door and as an escape route for smoke. There is little smoke when the temescal was being used because the fire was carefully tended and stoked with dry, flammable willow twigs. The men would enter the structure at the top, descending by a notched pole that acted as a ladder. They would then sit around the fire perspiring freely, using sweat sticks to scrape the moisture away. During this time they would sing and slap the ground before making a dash to the ocean or nearby pond to cool off (Menzies 1924:325).

The old or the sick and those infirmed with rheumatism made use of the *temescales* gaining some relief in the penetrating dry heat. Hunters used the *temescal* to mask all traces of their human scent allowing them to sneak up on large game unnoticed. They would rub themselves with pale white blossoms of ceanothus or fibrous soap plant creating a fine lather. Aromatic herbs were rubbed into the skin to further mask any trace of scent.

Stirgil. Bone sweatstick used by the Indians to scrape perspiration from the body while in the temescal.

Sweat houses were used primarily by men although women were reported to have used them in some villages. Small semi-circular sweat houses of wattle and mud were common and built into the side of a bank with slanting walls and a roof that allowed the rain to run off. The fire was built near a small door on the side of this mud structure (Hudson & Blackburn 1986:33-35).

Chumash men were said to have slept in the *temescales*. Various reasons have been given for this, perhaps they felt more secure, one early observer — Fages, has them bringing their bows and arrows within the lodge. The village hunters and fishermen may have stayed in the *temescal* to avoid consorting with women in the belief that having sexual intercourse would affect their hunting abilities. In any event the sweat lodge was routinely used once or twice daily for cleanliness and sudatory custom and was an integral part of Chumash life.

It is clear that the Chumash appreciated the comforts of a permanent home, well stocked with furnishings and that family groups lived together sharing the same hearth. The very fact that the Chumash were able to settle in one place and remain there for a number of years added to the richness of their culture and allowed for a stable lifestyle that encouraged the easy transference of traditional values.

CULTURE

A Look Back

THE COMPLEXITY OF Chumash culture was underestimated or simply ignored from the first European contact. The Spanish were more interested in conquering and converting the Chumash such that they had an almost total disregard for any native cultural values. Fortunately for us there was a tradition among these Europeans for travel writing and it is from these all too scarce sources that information passes to us. What history we have comes to us from ships logs, "diaries of the voyage", personal diaries and letter writing.

Still there exists a whole panoply of problems in reconstructing a true and living picture of Chumash culture, including confirming the accuracy of the information we already have. One problem is pointed up in the very definition of the word Chumash which is derived from the native word "Michumash" which was the name given to the inhabitants of Santa Cruz Islands by the Coastal Mainland people. This wider application of the word Chumash to the whole area is generally attributed to J.W. Powell in 1891 and is considered arbitrary in the sense that it was foisted on them. It is not arbitrary in that these people were very much alike genetically, descending from the same stock over a 10,000 year period. Their culture, values, religious beliefs, philosophy, language, and technology also bore a remarkable similarity.

Environment as a cultural factor should not be overlooked either. Climate, geography, flora, fauna and available water all directly relate to the way in which the Chumash lived and the manner in which they believed. The mild climate and relatively abundant food led to larger permanent villages along the coastal plain bordering the Channel. This led to a cultural unity in this area. From Ventura to Goleta along the Santa Barbara Channel, political, economic, and religious cultural values radiated outward. But despite this one should not suppose that the influence of these Coastal Mainland Chumash was homogeneous or paramount when considering the whole of Chumash territory.

Another factor to be considered when defining the Chumash is the problem of taking so much material from one source—Fernando Librado, a Harrington consultant. Still, his information can be evaluated in terms of internal consistency and agreement with historical sources.

Other problems in defining aspects of Chumash culture include the very passage of time as well as our own cultural differences from these peoples. There are tremendous gaps in our knowledge and we may never have the whole picture. And finally there are our own expectations and romance with native cultures which can obscure the fact that at times the life of the Chumash must have been a brutal and terrible existence.

Meanwhile the long process of reconstructing the past has begun. We know some of it. There is still more to learn.

CULTURE

VILLAGE LIFE AND SOCIAL ORGANIZATION

THE VILLAGE WAS the focal point of daily activity and the spiritual center of Chumash life. Many important activities took place in the village setting; the preparation of food, the manufacture of crafts, most games and sports, and the most significant ceremonies. There is little doubt that the Chumash took care in selecting a site to live and when living there took pride in its up keep.

Along the coast between present day Ventura and Goleta, the Chumash were most numerous. Many villages were permanently occupied although their population may have varied with the season depending on food resources. *Shisholop*, the village at the present site of Ventura, was reported to have had 400 people and 30 houses. Up the coast ranged fifty or more villages, some as large as 1000 inhabitants and 100 or more houses. Estuaries and sloughs at the mouths of creeks were favorite coastal village sites. On the Islands, particularly Santa Cruz and Santa Rosa, the villages tended to be near the shoreline rather than the mountainous interior. The Inland Chumash, living in an arid region and at a higher altitude were probably more nomadic, with less permanent and smaller villages due to their smaller food base.

Large or small, villages were planned around the same principles. The "design" of a village would include houses, including the chief's house, pathways leading between houses forming a kind of street in some larger villages, and a sweat house. Another important feature of the village was the storehouse or granary which might be located near the Chief's house or in a dry, well trafficked area away from rodents. To one side of the village was a flat cleared playing field for games, a ceremonial ground with a sacred enclosure called a *siliyik* and on high ground but within the environs of the village there was usually a cemetery.

The largest and best situated house in a village would be the house of the chief. It might hold his immediate family and his extended clan, usually sons and their families. Every village had at least one chief. The Chumash called him *Wot* and he was the moral authority over his people, dispensing justice as he saw fit. Some villages were reported to have more than one leader and some areas of the coast were so heavily populated that the chiefs of several villages would form a council with one being made *paqwot* or "big chief" (Hudson et al. 1977).

Still there were limits on the authority of the chief. Even though he ruled for life the village had final approval on his decisions such that in some ways his role was that of a figurehead. He was in charge of the ceremonial objects and costumes which were kept in a special place until the festivals. He also arranged for, furnished and paid the personnel who gave the ceremony and performed the dances.

The position of chief was inherited patrilineally and both men and women have been reported by Cabrillo and others as being *Wot*. A daughter might inherit the reins of power and thus continue the bloodline's high position.

The chief exercised his power over many areas of daily life, such as the gathering and dispensing of food and the allotment shelter. One of the duties of the chief was caring for the poor. It was also his duty to feed and entertain visitors, hence many Spanish diary accounts featured notes on the important people of a village and scant information on the poorer or less powerful members of the tribe.

Another duty of the chief was to declare war and to plan battles. These battles were generally for revenge, not for conquest. The reason for a war might stem from an insult from one village to the other, or from one chief to another. Perhaps the untimely death of a woman of one community who had married into another might bring on suspicions and accusations of unjust treatment from one community to another. Wars were fought for territorial reasons, one village invading the other's hunting or acorn gathering area was an often stated reason. Black mischief and petty theft were also said to be just reasons for war. The Chumash were not easily angered although they did have a strong sense of territory and would protect it when necessary.

Sometimes mock or formal battles were fought to settle a dispute. This civilized form of warfare usually involved a challenge as to the time and place a battle was to be fought. The Indians would arrive in full paint and wargear— bows, arrows, wooden spears with stone points and heavy wooden war clubs. Chert knives were used for fighting at close quarters. The Chumash would then throw feathers in the air and exchange war cries. Then one warrior would step forward and fire off a quiverful of arrows and when finished the other side would send someone forward to do the same. This continued until one or more were wounded or killed and the battle decided in favor of the side that held the field. In this way both sides satisfied their honor (Grant 1965:42-43).

The Chumash were monogamous with the exception of the village chief who could have more than one wife. Marriages were simple with a few words exchanged. The only grounds for divorce was adultery although separation and infidelity were apparently common. Sexual relations of the Chumash were expansive even shocking by European standards.

Births were primitive although they were significant enough to be attended by a shaman and verbally recorded by the village messenger. The pregnant woman would deliver the baby on her own into a hole filled with straw. She would then clean the newborn infant of the amniotic sack and blood, cutting the umbilical cord with a knife. She would then immediately break the cartilage in the nose of the infant to flattened it in accordance with custom.

Chumash society was a classed society with upper, middle and lower groups. A person's class depended on family relationships, on knowledge and skills, and on wealth. Most people, as would be expected, fell into the middle class. These were the people who were working members of society in good health and with skills such as basket making and hunting. Members of the village from the most important craft specialist groups, the shaman-doctors, the astrologer priests and the brotherhood of the canoe belonged to the upper class and were privileged in both position and wealth. They made up the ruling group and among them were all the important people: the *Wot*, the *Paha* who was an assistant to and appointed by the chief as master of ceremonies at festivals and the *Ksen* who was a messenger to the chief and reported directly to him. The *Ksen* would often travel from village to village collecting news and important information such as births and deaths. In one sense he was the eyes and ears of the chief (Hudson et al.,1977).

The poor Chumash, the lower class, were no doubt those of lesser abilities, the layabouts, the unskilled and the infirmed who didn't have family clans to help them.

The Chumash society was further stratified by craft guilds. There is evidence that a number of guilds existed — canoe builders,, basketry makers, bead making, hunting, woodworking and weapon makers to name some of the most obvious. It is thought that among them, the brotherhood of the canoe was probably the most powerful. These guilds operated on a profit motive and were very much like extended families (Hudson & Blackburn 1982:26).

Craft specialization encouraged the manufacture of more goods than could be used in one locale. This in turn led to an increase in trading between villages and between tribes, an activity that was common and on going throughout the year. With the easy flow of goods, local economies thrived and the Chumash way of life was not only sustained but flowered.

CULTURE

THE CHUMASH VILLAGES traded frequently among themselves. Barter for goods was sophisticated, with standardized sizes and quality of the goods both affecting the price. Trading helped to increase the diversity of goods that were available in any one area. Goods that were common on the coast might be scarce or unavailable inland, therefore trade was not only opportunistic but necessary. This routine trading of surplus articles, encouraged craft specialization leading to manufacturing sites on the coast and the Islands.

Chumash territory can be divided into three rough trading groups, Inland, Mainland Coast and Island. Trading no doubt occurred between certain individuals or villages where a relationship had been established. In this way, needs might be refined and a better relationship established between ordinarily disparate groups. Only a few individuals could account for a relatively large amount of trade between areas. One man might get used to dealing with a specific trading partner and would return every year to repeat the process.

A regional economy and network of trading sites and trails developed throughout southern California directly linking the Chumash with their neighbors and other tribes as far away as the Mojave desert near the Colorado River. The amount of goods traded was substantial and there were set patterns and times for trading to take place. The Chumash were in fact one of the richest tribes in California and probably supplied most of the shell bead money used in southern California.

This money was made from Olivella shells which were broken into pieces of roughly similar size, drilled with a chert drill and then strung on fiber string or sinew. The beads were then rounded to uniform size by rolling the strung pieces of shell back and forth on a sandstone surface. The standard unit of measure in Chumash territory and much of the south was a string of beads wrapped once around the hand.

The word Chumash is derived from the name Ventura Chumash called the Santa Cruz Island Indians: *michumash*, a word of multiple meanings one of which is, "those who make shell bead money." This shell bead money was used for a variety of purposes besides trade, including offerings at shrines and as payment for the dancers at festival time.

Between the Island and the Mainland Chumash there was heavy trafficking in trade goods. Goods traveling from the islands to the mainland were beads, shell jewelry, fishbones for beads, steatite, digging stick weights, ollas, otter and seal skins, chert knives and drills, baskets and sea lion meat. In turn the islanders got acorns, pine nuts, chia sage, islay (wild cherry) deer and rabbit skins (there were none on the islands) deer antlers for tools, bows and arrows, baskets, serpentine bowls (serpentine came from the San Rafael Mountains in the upper Santa Inés river area) and obsidian points (Davis 1974).

The Chumash traders would travel back and forth in their canoes, meeting at selected spots. Refugio Beach (*Qasil*), Santa Barbara Harbor (*Syuhtun*), Carpinteria (*Mishopshno*), and South of Ventura (*Shisholop*) were said to be important trading centers between these two groups. There was also much trading among villages up and down the coast. Just as the Coastal Chumash acted as intratribal middlemen, the Inland Chumash (Cuyama and Emigdiano) were brokers for the foreign tribes to the east, the Yokuts, the Kitanemuk, and the Mojaves. The Inland Chumash would come to the coast regularly to trade for fresh and dried fish, shellfish, starfish, baskets, steatite, chipped stone points, stone tools, and carved wooden vessels (Davis 1974).

The Chumash would travel north with trade goods for the Salinans giving them steatite which had originally come from the Island Gabrielino, wooden vessels, grooved stones that were perhaps net sinkers, jewelry including flat shell beads, columella beads, shell bead money and tubular serpentine (Baldwin n. d.). From the Yokuts to the east the Coastal Chumash received elk, deer, and antelope meat and skins, pottery, obsidian for points and knives, black pigment, carrizo sugar, pine nuts, anadromous fish, honeydew, wild tobacco, various herbs and salt. In return they gave shells beads, cowerie, clam, abalone, olivella, and limpet shells for making jewelry, asphaltum in small balls, or compressed in abalone shells, otter and seal pelts and white pigment (Davis 1974).

The Mojave, a tribe that inhabited the desert regions of inland California near the Colorado River would make a two week trip over the mountains into the central valley and then over to the coast to trade with the Chumash. High above they would see the giant condor gliding noiselessly on the wind, round and round. This would tell them they were near Chumash territory. They brought black woven cotton for blankets, fire-hardened pottery, and small balls of bright red hematite that the Chumash particularly liked for rock painting, body painting and for decorating a great variety of everyday objects. The Chumash gave them shell beads and jewelry, fiber and sinew rope, and asphaltum in return (Davis 1974).

CULTURE

THE CHUMASH WERE a fun loving people who set much store in music, dancing and games. They were avid gamblers, especially the women who would play for shell bead money, tossing dice across a flat coiled basket tray. Music served as simple entertainment and more significantly as an accompaniment to the religious dances at festivals. Guests were often entertained by dancing and festive music.

Father Crespí related in his diary that the Chumash were competitive in this regard with each village trying to outdo the next in presents and musical entertainment for the visitors; so much so that it was almost impossible for the explorers to beg off and get a good night's sleep.

> "In the afternoon the chief men came from each town, one after the other adorned according to their usage, painted and loaded with plumage and some hollow reeds in their hands, to the movement and noise of which they kept time with their songs and the cadence of the dance, in such good time and in such unison that it produced real harmony" (Bolton 1927:168).

John P. Harrington, recorded a number of Chumash songs on wax cylinders and aluminum discs. They present a unique and beautiful insight into Chumash music. The melodies and lyrics of Chumash songs are at once elemental and complex. In form and subject they are both humorous and quite serious making use of repetition, invocation, call and response, and lyrical chanting. The subjects of these songs cover many areas including gambling, power, love, mourning, morals and religion. Some are lullabies and children's songs. Many of these songs were sung by two or more people during festival dances and acted to tell a story or were sung as an invocation to the spiritual world (Walsh 1976:34).

The Chumash had a few favorite instruments to accompany this music. Flutes and whistles were numerous and were made of bone, wood and cane.

Flutes were like hollow tubes, open at both ends and with four, five or six holes as stops in the sides which when covered produced various high pitched musical notes. Whistles had two holes, one at the end (the other end was plugged with asphaltum) and one in the side. Whistles were made from the tibia (lower leg bone) of deer, from mountain lion bones or from hollow bird bones sometimes bound together like pan pipes. They were decorated with asphaltum and shell beads or incised with geometric patterns. The musicians sometimes wore them suspended by fiber strings from their necks (Hudson & Blackburn 1986: 349).

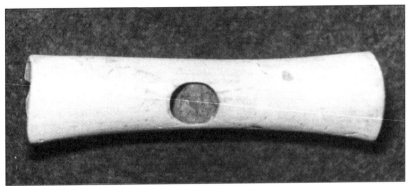

Bone Whistle with asphaltum plug. 4 inches.
Courtesy of Mission San Luis Obispo Museum.

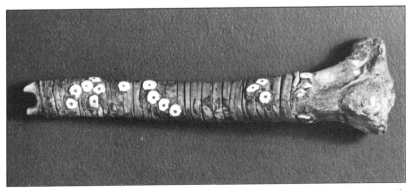

Deer tibia whistle with shell bead overlay. The
beads are laid on in such a way as to suggest
asterisms in the night sky at the time of the
winter solstice. See Crystals in the Sky.
Courtesy of the Ventura County Historical
Museum.

Deer tibia whistle. These ceremonial whistles from the shinbone of a deer produce a clear but shrill note. Courtesy of the Ventura County Historical Museum.

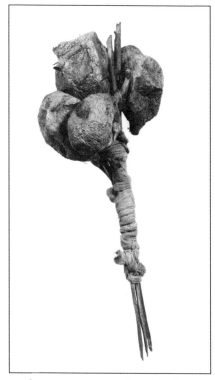

Ceonothus cocoon rattle collected in Cayucos, San Luis Obispo County by Henry Henshaw. Moth cocoons filled with pebbles are tied to three small sticks with string and a piece of cloth rag. Courtesy of the Smithsonian Institution.

Pan Pipe bird bone whistle with asphaltum plugs. Courtesy Mission San Luis Obispo.

The Chumash had a number of percussive type instruments. These included bullroarers (a small flat board that is swung around in the air over the head to make a low buzz), tap sticks (two sticks like drum sticks which when struck together make a clacking sound), split stick clappers which, when waved in the air correctly will produce a sharp clapping sound and rattles of various types (Hudson & Blackburn 1986).

Every village of size had a playing field. It was a wide level area that had been cleared of weeds and rocks and had the dirt packed down smooth from wear. A short fence of wood slats and tule matting surrounded this cleared surface marking the area of play. Games of kickball, marbles, shinny, archery and hoop and pole were played with great ability and much gambling on the outcome. Winning and losing depended on two things, skill and supernatural fate. The Chumash did not have a concept of luck as we know it. They believed in personal power and its interaction with other natural and supernatural forces. The stronger your magic the more you could influence the outcome of the game.

The hoop and pole game involved the rolling of a perforated stone disk on the ground inside a relatively small area. Players would then try to spear the hole at the center of the disc.

Shinny was a fast moving game that was played with a curved wooden bat that resembled a modern hockey stick in form and use. The puck was a ball of wood that was longer than it was wide and tapered at the ends. It was batted or struck around the playing field with the stick in an effort to score a goal at the opposite end of the field.

The Chumash were great gamblers and lovers of games of chance. One game was played by holding a small piece of wood in the hand behind the back and then having the opposite player guess which hand held the stick. Shell bead money, trinkets, jewelry or precious objects were wagered. Women tossed walnut shell dice on to a flat coiled basket tray in a game of chance. The dice were made from one half of a black walnut shell hollowed out and filled with asphaltum, thus each die had a flat and a round side. The flat side of the die was decorated with shell beads impressed in the asphaltum and the round side sometimes had painted designs in red ochre (Hudson & Blackburn 1986:405).

CULTURE

THE THREE WORLDS

There is this world in which we live, but there is also one above us and one below us. The world below is where the *nunasis* live. Here where we live is the center of our world — it is the biggest island. And there are two giant serpents that hold up our world from below. When they are tired they move, and that causes earthquakes. The world above is sustained by the great Eagle who by stretching his wings causes the phases of the moon.

THE MAKING OF MAN

After the flood, the Coyote of the Sky, Sun, Moon, Morning Star and the Great Eagle were discussing how they were going to make man. Coyote announced that there would be people in this world and they should all be in his image since he had the finest hands. Lizard was there also, but he just listened night after night and said nothing. At last Coyote won the argument. The next day they all gathered around a beautiful table-like rock that was there in the sky, a white rock of such fine texture that whatever touched it left an exact impression. Coyote was about to stamp his hand down on the rock when Lizard, who had been standing silently just behind, quickly reached out and pressed a perfect handprint into the rock himself. Coyote was enraged and wanted to kill Lizard, but Lizard ran down into a deep crevice and so escaped. And Eagle and Sun approved of Lizard's actions, so what could Coyote do? They say that the mark is still impressed on that rock in the sky. If Lizard had not done what he did, we might have hands like a coyote today.

Courtesy of the Smithsonian Institution, N.A.A. Collected by John Peabody Harrington from Maria Solares (Box 5, fd. 3) and (Box 137). Courtesy of Thomas C. Blackburn, *December's Child, A Book of Chumash Oral Narratives*. University of California Press, 1975.

CULTURE

RELIGION
COSMOLOGY

THE CHUMASH BELIEVED in a great and powerful universe, full of mystery and supernatural forces. Reality was a delicate equilibrium between a number of opposing forces and a place in which humans played an essential role in the balance of all things. Their world was dominated by natural elemental forces, earth, wind, fire, water, and by supernatural entities of three types, Gods of the Upper World, the "First People" and the *Nunashish* (beings of the Lower World). The Chumash were ever-conscious that power was everywhere, in themselves, with the animals, the plants, the elementals, above in the Sun, the Moon, the Morning Star and the Evening Star and below in an inverted world of dark, malevolent beings. Their daily activities were performed with this in mind.

Power was neutral. All things except inanimate objects in the Middle World had the ability to tap the power that had been scattered in the universe when it was created. It could be used for both good and bad purposes. It was the user of that power and the path taken that gave power its positive and negative aspects. Because power was amoral it was therefore dangerous and there was all the more reason to appoint a special elite group to access and control it (Blackburn 1975).

The Chumash believed that the universe was divided into three worlds each laid on top of the other like three coins stacked in a dark void. Upper, Middle, and Lower Worlds were flat and circular, connected and yet separate. The three worlds of the Chumash universe were not infinite but had set boundaries that could be traveled if a person was possessed of the correct rituals, power objects, visionary abilities, spirit helpers and above all the the right skills to move among unpredictable supernatural beings.

Above in the Upper World (*'Alapay*) lived the Gods of the Moon and the Sun and with them, the First People (supernatural beings with the human attributes of will, reason and emotion). The Gods of the Upper World were the most powerful entities in the Universe. Chumash myth has it that the

Upper world is supported by the wings of a giant eagle of great strength. The cosmic sweep of the eagle's wings act as a great motor pushing the heavenly bodies inevitably along their paths.

In the Middle World (*'Itiashup*) is the earth, a flat island suspended between Upper and Lower Worlds and surrounded by a great sea. It was called the "world of the people". Long before man was created this Middle World was inhabited by the First People until a cataclysmic flood changed the face of the universe. This flood brought death to some of the *Nunashish* of the Lower World and a great transformation to the First People, some of whom stayed in the Middle World as elemental forces (water, thunder, wind) and as animal and plant spirits. Others of the First People ascended to join the celestial beings, "Sky People" of the Upper World.

With the Flood came the creation of Man who made his home the in the Middle World. Man was created when a council of beings from the Upper World, the Sun who was male, the Moon who was female, The Morning Star (Venus), the Sky Coyote, Lizard, and the Great Eagle met and discussed how man would be made. With man came life and death which led to the Chumash belief that all earthly things are in flux in a natural cycle of reincarnation.

The Lower World (*C'oyinashup*) is the realm of dark beings, described as misshapen, capable of evil mischief and great harm to human beings. They slip into the Middle World at night and can take on the form of a human or other malevolent guises (Blackburn 1975).

CULTURE

AMONG THE CHUMASH were shamans. These men and women held great power and employed the secret ritual practices and esoteric knowledge to tap the supernatural power all around them. The astronomer priests, one type of shaman interpreted the cosmos for the benefit of all the Chumash people.

This ability to interpret the direction of heavenly bodies was especially relevant to the Chumash because their world was seen as being in constant flux. The ability to interpret the movements of the sun, moon and stars and utilize their power to influence the course of cosmic events was the key role of the astronomer priests, called *'alchuklash*. Their immediate concern was for the continued balance and proper alignment of the forces in the universe. These shamans held great power in both the religious and the political spheres, were looked up to and at times even feared by the ordinary people.

The *'alchuklash* were astronomers and astrologers studying both the heavens and the effect the heavens had on the life and destiny of the Chumash people. The Chumash were intensely interested in and aware of the movements of the cosmos. Many of their rituals were intimately linked to the heavens above and they closely followed the phases of the moon as well as the rising, setting and declination of the sun (Hudson & Underhay 1978).

Their world was divided by the four cardinal points of the compass. South was called *minawan*, east *'ulop*, west *wotoko*. North, called *miwalaqsh* by the Chumash, was also their name for the north star (Polaris). It was also the name given to the ceremonial sunstaff, a ritual object consisting of a painted stone disk with a hole at the center through which a short wooden staff was placed. This staff was used during the winter solstice ceremony, a time when the sun would be at its furthest south and lowest declination (Hudson & Underhay 1978).

The Chumash called the sun *Kakunupmawa*. A large festival honoring the sun took place at the time of the winter solstice. Preparations for this festival, including the making of ceremonial regalia and astronometric projections of the actual winter solstice by the shamans were done throughout the fall. The ritual sequence of this festival, as told by Fernando Librado and recorded by J. P. Harrington, has it that on the first day all debts from the previous year were cleared. On the second day a sunstaff about a foot and a half tall was erected at the center of the ceremonial ground by a priest and twelve helpers. The perforated stone atop the sunstaff was painted green or blue to resemble a sand dollar. One Chumash myth suggests that the sand dollar represents the sun and that as the sun traverses the heaven during the day it will stop and rest, hiding momentarily in the the holes of the sand dollar. The sunstaff stone was sometimes incised with rays or geometric designs representing the sun and or possibly the cardinal points. To release the power of the sunstaff, the stone was tapped and ceremonial words were spoken by the *paha* (master of ceremonies) and then sun was symbolically pulled in a northward direction (Hudson et al. 1977).

Sun Staff. Wooden staff surmounted by a perforated steatite disk. Used during Kakunupmawa, the festival of the sun during winter solstice. Incised marking on the top edge are thought to mark the inclination of the sun and four cardinal points of the compass (Hudson et al.,1977).

Another equally important time for the Chumash was *Hutash*, the harvest festival. *Hutash* was the month of the harvest late in the summer (August or September), when the acorns had been collected and stored. It was a time of rejuvenation and celebration of the abundance of the earth and the triumph of love. It was during *Hutash* that the preparation for the winter solstice were begun. The Chumash word *Hutash* had many meanings but all were inter-related. *Hutash* meant the earth and the evening star (Venus) probably because it appeared in the sky during the month of the festival.

Like most harvest festivals worldwide this was a time of thanksgiving and celebration of the earth as the source and mother of all food. And like many festivals it was a time to be serious and a time to have fun. Games, sports, gambling (especially at night) and dances with musical accompaniment were commonplace and ongoing during the five or six days of the festival. *Hutash* was a festival that drew people from a wide area and thus became a time when trading flourished not only because of harvest surpluses but because of the known difficulties of traveling during the upcoming winter (Hudson et al. 1977).

Many of the rituals performed during festivals took place on the ceremonial ground, a flat cleared area not unlike the gaming field. Around the ceremonial area was a fence made of tule matting or woven boughs. Sometimes the jaw of a whale painted with red ochre would mark the edge of the ceremonial ground letting people know that a ceremony or demonstration of power was to occur in the near future. Within the ceremonial ground was the *Siliyik*, the sacred enclosure where only certain people were allowed — the *'antap* dancers, and musicians performing the ceremony. The *Siliyik* was semicircular area enclosed by high fence of tule matting so that no one could see inside. The entrance faced east away from the eyes of the people gathered to watch the dancing. They sat on tule mats at the western edge of the ceremonial ground in a large half circle of many fireplaces each of which was designated for a specific family or group of visitors (Hudson & Blackburn 1986:50-65).

Long feathered banners were hung around the sacred enclosure at festival time. Some of the most beautiful workmanship went into these feathered banners of the Chumash. Raptor feathers were frequently used.

Feathered poles that usually stood on high ground were brought down and used in Sun Ceremony. These feathered poles were used as protective shrines, the Chumash believing that the seed crop would grow better if beads and chia were offered to the shrine. They were about the size of a nearly grown boy, painted black and surmounted with plumage of a raven or an eagle. The type of feathers, the color of paint and the design of such poles almost certainly had significance for the Chumash. Subtle differences in design might have vastly different meanings. One type of feathered pole signified a crop shrine, still another demarcated the place where a chief would sit a festival time (Hudson & Blackburn 1986).

Dances were more than entertainment, they were an integral part of religious ceremonies. Music and song accompanied the dancers who were dressed in elaborate costumes of woven skirts, shell beads, and feather headdresses. Each dance had a specific sequence of steps, direction, music and songs. Many dances were directed towards a particular animal or supernatural being. For example the Bear dance honored an animal admired for its strength, and the Swordfish dance was performed in appreciation of a fish the Chumash believed had mystical abilities to drive whales ashore.

Festivals were also a time when the 'antap could meet, confer and exchange news that concerned the ruling elite. The many shamans and chiefs decorated in full body paint and ritual paraphernalia gathered together for the serious business of correcting the alignment of the cosmos and balancing the power of the spheres would certainly have been impressive. For the ordinary person the importance of such events could not be overlooked.

Shamans were integral in a person's acquisition of power. If a person wished to utilize power, a dream helper was needed. A shaman guided the secret

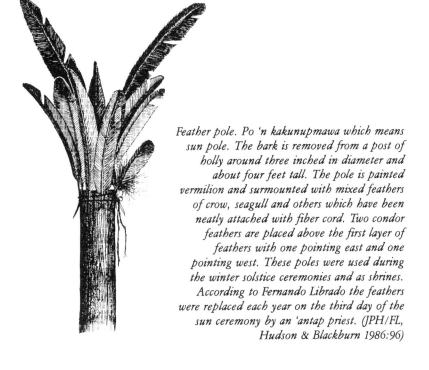

Feather pole. Po 'n kakunupmawa which means sun pole. The bark is removed from a post of holly around three inched in diameter and about four feet tall. The pole is painted vermilion and surmounted with mixed feathers of crow, seagull and others which have been neatly attached with fiber cord. Two condor feathers are placed above the first layer of feathers with one pointing east and one pointing west. These poles were used during the winter solstice ceremonies and as shrines. According to Fernando Librado the feathers were replaced each year on the third day of the sun ceremony by an 'antap priest. (JPH/FL, Hudson & Blackburn 1986:96)

Feathered dance stick made with black crow feathers and white wild geese feathers. Carried in the hand while dancing (Hudson & Blackburn 1985:206).

ritual and administered *toloache*, a hallucinatory drink made from jimson weed (*Datura wrightii*). This alkali based poison (scopolamine and atropine) induced a hallucinatory dream state, either waking or coma-like during which a person would meet by sign or recognition his dream helper. The power of that dream helper could then be utilized in the future. Praying, making offerings and fasting accompanied the trance. This elaborate ritual might be done several times or only once in a lifetime. A person's dream helper could be any one of a number of supernatural spirits inhabiting the universe: First People, celestial bodies, natural forces, plants and animals. Steatite effigies were the symbolic manifestations of these dream helpers although not all steatite effigies were dream helpers. Nor were all dream helpers effigies. Such a talisman or *'atishwin* was highly prized and closely protected, for loss of this personal object would mean the loss of the power that was so essential in Chumash life (Hudson & Underhay 1978).

Many California Indian tribes made use of charmstones, small cylindrical stones with tapered ends rather like plummet stones. Chumash shamans used these ritual objects for a variety of purposes including curing the sick, making oneself invisible to arrows, for sorcery and to bring rain. Shamans might also employ large quartz crystals which were sometimes attached to wands and

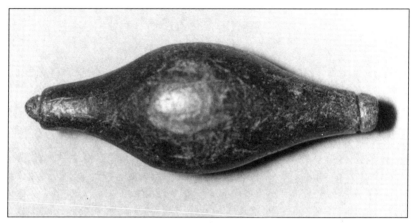

*Charmstone. This steatite example is about
three inches in length. Courtesy of Mission
San Luis Obispo Museum.*

*Perforated eagle talon talisman worn around
the neck for good luck.*

were associated with rainmaking. Other talismans included various animal parts such as bear claws, bird talons, rattlesnake skulls, and bits of human hair. These talismans were generally worn around the neck and signified specific powers (Hudson & Blackburn 1986).

Shamans served many vital functions in the life of the Chumash but were also viewed with some ambivalence. Shamans could possess more than one dream helper and were therefore seen as more powerful than ordinary people. They were specialists using their manifold and esoteric skills in various specific disciplines. They were present at births and deaths. They named children, predicted the future and influenced the course and nature of the weather. They cured illnesses by blowing smoke, by singing, by dancing and by ritual use of herbs. They were diviners and sorcerers; some could be possessed by a bear spirit which would give them great strength and allow them congress with bears. They could travel abroad, moving between realms and around the "world of the people" with a supernatural ability. They could create "human simulacra, children that seem normal but have only a brief life span" and above all they possessed the superior ability to control external events (Blackburn 1975:40).

One of the most important occupations among shamans was that of the medicine man. Experienced with datura, curative tree bark and medicinal herbs, these shaman doctors would treat the ill by summoning powers and sucking the disease from the patient's body by means of a steatite or bird bone tube. There were also herb doctors and pipe doctors.

Native medicine was holistic in nature and reasonably effective. The Chumash would treat themselves for minor aches and pains with medicinal plants. Bay leaves were used to treat headaches, sage for flu, elderberry for colds and fever and willow bark for toothache. Curing stones, a type of talisman made of steatite or serpentine and resembling incised pendants, were prized possessions. They were placed against the head of the sick person for their curative powers. A heated steatite comal was used in the fashion of a hot water bottle to soothe sore muscles (Hudson & Blackburn 1986).

Another sacred place was the cemetery. It was often set to one side of the village on a slight rise. The area of the cemetery was marked with stone slabs or a wooden fence and was high enough to be called a "high stockade" by Longinos Martinez in 1792 (Simpson 1961:52).

Graves were marked by stone slabs, wooden planks, wood grave poles or by the rib bones of whales. Stone slabs were incised and painted with red, black and white. Wooden planks were painted with black and white squares or other designs. Painted poles as tall as three or four times the height of the stone or wooden planks were erected over the grave site. A tall pole and profuse decoration probably denoted the grave of an eminent person or chief.

The ribs or other large bones of whales were erected, laid horizontally across, or even placed within the grave as a lining. Harrington noted the existence of some square wooden planks, perhaps grave markers painted with a black circle, a symbol associated with the swordfish dance and mourning ceremony of the Santa Cruz Island Chumash. Grave poles were decorated with paint and symbolic objects and or possessions highly esteemed by the deceased. A fisherman might have an oar suspended from his pole, a woman could be denoted by a hanging basket, a hunter by bows and arrows (Hudson & Blackburn 1986:69-78).

Burial involved a number of ritual practices. The body was first carried to the sacred enclosure where a wake with singing, dancing and a large fire took place during the night. The body was then carried to the cemetery amidst much lamentation by the relatives and other mourners. The deceased was then buried in the flexed position, knees roped together against the chest and placed in the grave with the face down. Then his personal objects, effigies, steatite bowls, beads, flint knives, charmstones, wands, pipes, bone whistles were placed in the grave. Of course not every person would have such a wealth of objects.

There is evidence that sometimes these personal objects were deliberately broken and scattered in the grave. Fernando Librado has said that effigies, like all power objects were useless once the owner has died (Hudson, Timbrook & Rempe 1978).

A type of mourning ceremony was conducted at the time of burial. There was also a ceremony held once every few years for all the people who had died in the interim. It would be planned several years in advance and took place during *Hutash* the harvest festival (Hudson et al. 1977).

Grave marker   Hudson & Blackburn 1986.

CULTURE

LANGUAGE

THERE ARE NO fluent speakers of any of the Chumashan languages living today. The smattering of language we have of their speech comes from word lists collected by early researchers. These lists contain descriptions of terrain, references to animals, names for plant life, and intimate knowledge of the elements, water, wind, and sky. Like most languages, the Chumash dialects were expressive of the natural environment in which the Indians lived.

Spoken from deep in the throat and off the tip of the tongue, these native languages were expansive enough to cover a wide range of sounds from strong gutterals, glottal stops and clicking noises to the halting and beautiful words of ritual songs of power. To the Spanish these languages must have seemed strange and awkward when compared to their own mellifluous latinate tongue. But to the Chumash, language could invoke high Gods and powerful spirit helpers to move the world. It could also be used to communicate in everyday activities, to teach a child, to sing, to tell stories. For the Chumash the very balance of the universe was connected to the spoken word. There was no written language.

Kroeber divided the Chumashan language into eight dialects: Obispeño, Santa Ynez, Cuyama, Emigdiano, Barbareño, Purísimeño, Ventureño, and Island. He noted them as derived from the Hokan superfamily, one of the most widely used in California, and as being related by root words to Pomo, Salinan, Esselen, Yuman, Yanan, and Shastan. Kroeber's divisions within Chumash territory were as much geographic as linguistic in nature. Researchers in the Chumashan languages and there were many both before and after Kroeber, agree with his list of eight dialects with some modifications.

Recent workers in this field with the help of the voluminous Harrington notes have decided that the eight Kroeber "dialects" were in reality distinct but related languages with their own dialectical subdivisions. Harrington was knowledgeable in Mainland Coast dialects and made accurate phonetic transcriptions of them into English. From his work it has been determined that there were two dialectical subdivisions of Island Chumash, two of Barbareño, and four Ventureño dialects (Applegate 1978).

Many of the placenames used today reflect their origins in the Chumashan languages. Pismo Beach was *pismu '*, Lompoc, *lompo '* and Nipomo was *nipumu '*, for example.

Harrington reviewed many of the early word lists and correlated them with his own information which included a 300 page grammar, a 3000 page dictionary and thousands of notes on Chumash phonetics, diction and lexicography. He collected more than 400 placenames and over 150 village names. Sadly, when he was doing his research in the early years of this century there were very few native speakers still alive. Consequently, present understanding of the many dialects and placenames is imperfect. Nevertheless, what has been saved through his work and the work of others, opens a window onto the unique culture of the Chumash (Walsh 1976).

CULTURE

ROCK ART

ROCK PAINTINGS ARE found in shallow sandstone caves and sheltered overhangs throughout much of Chumash territory. These extraordinary paintings are perhaps their finest achievement. Here is their voice and written language. Here is power made visible.

To our imagination these unexplained images resemble strange anthropomorphic creatures, abstract psychic tracings or even celestial maps. The paintings are as profound as they are mysterious, and even to this day they are the least understood area of Chumash studies. Nevertheless, some important work in the past two decades by Campbell Grant, Travis Hudson, Ernest Underhay, and Georgia Lee has given us a basis for understanding these complex expressions of Chumash culture.

The Chumash chose to place their pictograph sites near permanent water, in most cases in the natural cavities found in large rock formations. Here they painted complex images onto the hidden underbelly of rock outcrops. They sometimes chose to paint in caves hidden away by brush and foliage and sometimes these pictographs are found deep in worn crevices out of the reach of wind and water.

Some extraordinary rock art sites are found in the coastal areas but numerically the greater amount of sites are in the interior, particularly the Cuyama and Emigdiano areas. Here are found some spectacular paintings with expanded composite images painted over a number of years and at one site some five color designs.

Rock art exists at scattered sites over much of the western United States but nowhere as complex and unique as the images left by the Chumash. Stylistically Chumash rock art differs from neighboring tribes and even within the geography of the Chumash world there is much differentiation in both the style of the images and the method of creating them (Grant 1965).

Chumash rock paintings were probably created and viewed by a few persons of power, perhaps Chumash shamans. Although the sites were probably

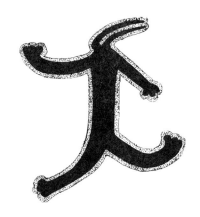

"Coyote" Painted Rock on Carrizo Plains.
Courtesy Bob Nichols.

known and even accessible to the ordinary person, they were feared as places of evil mystery. The common Chumash may even have been able to understand some of the dominant images utilized by the artists, certainly their knowledge would be greater than ours. The very nature of the site known as Painted Rock in San Luis Obispo County, being the only rock formation in a flat dry area and a focal point for local animal life, suggests that any hunter passing that way would not miss it or at the least know its purpose and something of the beauty there. This site is very close to the boundary of Chumash and Yokut territory and was used for a meeting and gathering place for trading and festivals by both tribes. To endow unusual rock formations with a special power and significance was common among the Chumash. Such sites were said to be earthly transformations of the "First People" and very often selected as pictograph sites (Lee 1984).

Making an age determination on the majority of the rock art sites in Chumash territory is difficult. Such radiocarbon testing would mean gathering a substantial amount of paint, thereby destroying the site. It has been variously estimated that most of the sites are probably within one thousand years of the present date, a period corresponding roughly with the golden age of Chumash culture (Grant 1965). Many of the sites have overpainting with a more recent style, masking older forms and some are painted near cupules (pit and groove petroglyphs) from a more primitive time. Thus some sites obviously have a longer history. Cupules are an ancient art form originating in

Asia and may have been used by the Chumash to mark boundaries or as birth or death records. Cupules may also have some connection to fertility rites or to the practice of native medicine. Cupules could also be an independent invention by the Chumash (Lee 1984).

It is not uncommon for Chumash rock art sites to have more than one style represented among the images. Even within one "style" there can be both representational and abstract images. A linear red style of painting seems to be the most common although linear black and white drawings are numerous. Many have dots, finger ticks and geometric designs. The Chumash artists were fond of combining parts of different animals to create strange and wonderful anthropomorphic creatures. There are also many examples of hand prints, pinwheels, chevrons, stars, and various aquatic and bird forms (Grant 1965).

The colors chosen by the Chumash for their rock paintings were from the landscape around them. They were earth colors, red, black, white, yellow, blue and green. Red was far and away the most common with blue and green much rarer. Of the colors the Chumash used, black, red and white are typical. Red lasts the longest, due partially to the fact that this pigment seems to be readily absorbed into the stone surface on which it was painted. Even so, considering the age of some of these paintings their colors are remarkably bright to this day.

Red pigment was made from iron oxide and is sometimes called hematite. This iron compound has many of the same hues as human blood with shades ranging from a flat brownish rust color to bright red. Yellow to orange pigments were also an iron oxide compound called limonite. The color of iron oxide varies depending on the amount of oxygen bonding. Exposure to a flame will of course heighten the redness. White pigment varies from a chalky yellow to a purer white that was obtained from diatomaceous clay found in scattered deposits on the mainland coast. White was also a color associated by the Chumash with celestial bodies. Black pigment was ash or oak charcoal, soot, oxidized manganese, or charcoaled graphite. Some shades of hematite probably came from southern California tribes with the purest black coming from the Yokuts to the east (Hudson 1982), (Grant 1975).

Paint was a traded commodity and came in small cakes much the way soap does today. Pigments were first mined and then perhaps heat treated. Next, they were crushed to powder, mixed with water and binding medium to make a thick paste and finally formed into convenient-sized bars and left to dry. These paint cakes were kept in small leather bags and carried to the site for ready use. Paint was applied with brushes made from yucca, soaproot or duck feathers. Finger and handpainting was also used as well as direct application on the stone surface with the paint cake. Small stone mortars and pestles were used to grind the caked pigments. Cupules, often found near rock art sites, may have served as paint mortars although many cupules are on vertical surfaces and obviously have another function. The Chumash also used wooden bowls as well as mortars made from large fish vertebrae to hold paint. Ground to a fine powder, pigments were mixed with a binder the composition of which is unknown. Various substances have been suggested including water, egg whites, animal fat or possibly the sticky white juice obtained from milkweed plants (Grant 1965),(Lee 1984). The Plains Indians commonly used cactus sap from the ubiquitous *Nopales* as a binding medium. Prickly pear leaves could be split lengthwise and used as palettes on which paint might be mixed directly (Morrow 1975:36).

The meaning of these pictographs is possibly bound up in shamanistic ritual. The Shaman, seeking the meaning of power in the universe to gain some control over dangerous forces loose in the world, would work magic. These paintings are the means by which power was utilized and made real.

It is possible that the "meaning" of these paintings varied from site to site or that their significance changed over time. Perhaps their "meaning" was handed down within the *'antap* organization with some symbols being universally recognized and others being obscure or idiosyncratic to that artist and that site. Whatever their meaning, they were important to the psychic well-being of the Chumash and even today they represent a powerful if mysterious aspect of reality. One should never forget that what the paintings represent to us with our culturally biased interpretation of art does not apply to the Chumash. The designs are not signs of our own existence, but images from the Chumash mind, whose belief systems, world view and very semiotics would necessarily be vastly different from our own. Hence, any interpretation of the Chumash mind set and extrapolation of meaning from these pictographs must be seen as difficult at best.

It is evident from the literature extant that these rock paintings are representative of six areas of "meaning" within the Chumash world view.

One: That they were a mythic links to the Chumash past featuring stylized mythological characters such as Sky Coyote, Lizard, and Bear.

Two: That they have astronomical significance and were created for use in shamanistic power rituals.

Three: That they are celestial or terrain maps.

Four: That they were created under a drug induced trance during vision questing and have a proprietary and internal significance to the artist only.

Five: That they are a record of significant events.

Six: That they are symbolic representations of cultural ideas, beliefs, natural laws, or other abstract concepts, such as time, death, or fertility.

These six categories are not mutually exclusive and together they may represent as close as we could come to an interpretation of these extraordinary graphic records (Lee 1984),(Grant 1965),(Hudson & Conti 1984),(Alioto 1984).

The rock paintings of the Chumash are the most spectacular of their art forms but they were an exceptional people and their concern for craftsmanship and art within the meaning of their own world view was substantial. Most of their crafts reflected this concern. Every object had a practical and spiritual side. To do art was to do magic. It was a profoundly religious act for these people. Baskets, feathered banners, canoes, weapons, effigies, even the small personal items used for grooming all got special "artistic" attention. It is a tragedy how little of this legacy remains to inform our lives.

Even now many rock paintings are being eroded by wind and water or savaged by vandals. Just as much of what was once Chumash has slipped away into the past, so too will these go. Historical sites are being built upon and otherwise disturbed. Much has been done and continues to be done by scholars and researchers to retrieve and enliven this heritage. The actual living descendants of the Chumash are working hard in this area too, trying to preserve and resurrect their own past. All of this allows the continuance of our knowledge. This is all to the good, for such a legacy is hard and terrible thing for our world to lose.

BIBLIOGRAPHY

Alioto, Joseph T., et al. 1984. *Papers on Chumash Rock Art.* San Luis Obispo County Archaeological Society #12.

Anderson, Eugene N. A Revised, 1978. *Annotated Bibliography of the Chumash and Their Predecessors.* Ballena Press.

Angel, Myron. 1883. *History of San Luis Obispo, California.* Thompson & West.

Applegate, Richard. 1975. *Index of Chumash Placenames.* SLOCAS Occasional Papers 9.

Applegate, Richard. 1975. *The Datura Cult Among the Chumash*, JCA 2(1).

Applegate, Richard. 1978. *'Atishwin: The Dream Helper in South-Central California*, Anthropological Papers 13. Ballena Press.

Baldwin, Mary Alice, N. d. *Archaeological Evidence of Cultural Continuity From Chumash To Salinan Indians In California.* S.L.O. County Archaeological Society Occasional paper No# 6.

Baxter, Don J. 1970. *Missions of California.* Pacific Gas and Electric Company.

Bean, Lowell John & King, Thomas F., eds. 1974. *'Antap; California Indian Political and Economic Organization.* Ballena Press.

Bean, Walton E. 1973. *California: An Interpretive History.* McGraw-Hill Book Company.

Beers, C. David, et al. 1975. *Papers on the Chumash.* San Luis Obispo County Archaeological Society #9.

Blackburn, Thomas C. 1975. *December's Child, A Book of Chumash Oral Narratives.* University of California Press.

Bolton, Herbert Eugene. 1916, 1925. *Spanish Exploration in the Southwest 1542-1706.* Scribners.

  1927. *Fray Juan Crespí, Missionary Explorer on the Pacific Coast.* University of California Press.

  1930. *Anza's California Expeditions.* University of California Press.

  1931. *Font's Complete Diary: A Chronicle of the Founding of San Francisco.* University of California Press.

Brandes, Ray. 1970. *The Costansó Narrative of the Portolá Expedition.* Hogarth Press.

Chapman, Charles Edward. 1916. *The Founding of Spanish California.* The Macmillan Co.

Cleland, Robert Class. 1930. *A History of California, The American Period.* Macmillan Co.

Dana, R. H. 1937. *Two years Before the Mast.* Collier & Son.

Davis, James T. 1974. *Trade Routes and Economic Exchange Among the Indians of California.* Ballena Press.

Davis, W. H. 1929. *Seventy Five Years in California.* Howell.

Dawson, L. & Deetz, J. 1964. *Chumash Indian Art.* University of California Santa Barbara.

Dawson, L. & Deetz, J. 1965. *A Corpus of Chumash Basketry.* University of California Los Angeles.

Engelhardt, Zephyrin. 1923. *Santa Barbara Mission.* The James H. Barry Co.

Gerow, Bert A. 1974. *Co-Traditions and Convergent Trends In Prehistoric California,* S.L.O. County Archaeological Society Occasional paper No# 8.

Glassow, Michael A. 1977. *Archaeological Overview of the Northern Channel Islands California.* National Park Service.

Grant, Campbell. 1965. *The Rock Paintings of the Chumash.* University of California Press.

Greenwood, Roberta S. 1972. *9000 Years of Prehistory At Diablo Canyon, San Luis Obispo County California.* S.L.O. County Archaeological Society Occasional Paper No# 7.

Heizer, Robert F. 1975. *Handbook of North American Indians, Volume 8, California.* Smithsonian Institution. 1975.

Heizer, Robert F. & Bowman, J. N. 1967. *Anza and the Northwest Frontier of New Spain.* Southwest Museum.

Heizer, Robert F. & Elsasser, Albert B. 1980. *The Natural World of the California Indians.* University of California Press.

Heizer, Robert F. & Whipple, M.A. 1971. *The California Indians, 2nd edition.* University of California Press.

Heizer, Robert F. (ed.) 1974. *They Were Only Diggers, A Collection of Articles from California Newspapers 1851-1866, on Indian and White Relations.* Ballena Press.

Hemert, Robert, and Adan Teggart, eds. 1910. *The Narrative of the Portolá Expedition of 1769-1770 by Miguel Costansó.* Publications of the Academy of Pacific Coast History.

Heye, George. 1921. *Certain Artifacts from San Miguel Island, California.* Museum of the American Indian Heye Foundation.

Hoover, Robert L. 1971. *Chumash Typologies For Dating and Computer Analysis.* S.L.O. County Archaeological Society Occasional paper No# 2.

1973. *Chumash Fishing Equipment.* San Diego Museum of Man.

1974. *Some Observations on Chumash Prehistoric Stone Effigies.* Journal of California Anthropology, Spring.

Hudson, Dee T. 1974. *Chumash Archery Equipment.* San Diego Museum of Man.

Hudson, Travis & Blackburn, Thomas C. 1982-1986. *The Material Culture of the Chumash Interaction Sphere, Volumes 1-4,* Santa Barbara Museum of Natural History, Ballena Press.

Hudson, Travis, et al. 1978. *Tomol: Chumash Watercraft as Described in the Ethnographic Notes of John P. Harrington.* Ballena Press.

Hudson, Travis & Ernest Underhay. 1978. *Crystals in the Sky: An Intellectual Odyssey Involving Chumash Astronomy, Cosmology and Rock Art.* Ballena Press.

Hudson, Travis, et al. 1977. *Eye of the Flute: Chumash Traditional History and Ritual as Told by Fernando Librado Kitsepawit to John P. Harrington.* Santa Barbara Museum of Natural History.

Kirsch, R. & Murphy, W.S. 1967. *Witnesses to the California Experience, 1542-1906.* West of the West. Dutton & Co.

Kroeber, A.L. 1976. *Handbook of the Indians of California.* Dover Publications, Inc.

Landberg, Lief C.W. 1965. *The Chumash Indians of Southern California.* Southwest Museum.

McCall & Perry eds., et al. 1982. *The Chumash People, Materials for Teachers and Students,* The Santa Barbara Museum of Natural History.

Menzies, Archibald. 1924. *Journal of the Vancouver Expedition.* Edited by Alice Eastwood. CHS-Q 2:264-340.

Morrow, Mabel. 1975. *Indian Rawhide; An American Folk Art.* Univ. of Oklahoma Press.

Nidever, George. 1973. *The Life and Adventures of a Pioneer of California Since 1934. In, Original Accounts of the Lone Woman of San Nicolas Island,* Robert Heizer and Albert Elsasser, eds. Ballena Press.

Orr, Phil C. 1956. *Customs of the Canalino.* Santa Barbara Museum of natural History #6.

Priestley, Herbert, ed. 1937. *A Historical, Political, and Natural Description of California by Pedro Fages,* Soldier of Spain. U. C. Berkeley.

Reddell, Dan. 1970. *Harrigan Site-Shell Beach.* S.L.O. County Archaeological Occasional paper No # 1.

Reichlen, Henry & Heizer, R. F. 1964. *The Scientific Expedition of Leon De Cessac To California,* 1877-1879. University of California.

Richie, C.F. & Hager, R.A. 1973. *The Chumash Canoe.* San Diego Museum of Man.

Rogers, David Banks. 1929. *Prehistoric Man of the Santa Barbara Coast.* Santa Barbara Museum of Natural History.

Sandos, James A. 1987. *Levantamiento! The 1924 Chumash Uprising.* The Californians pgs. 9-20.

Simpson, L. B. 1938. *California in 1792, The Expedition of J. Longinos Martinez.* Huntington Library.

Squibb, Paul. 1984. *Captain Portolá in San Luis Obispo County in 1769.* Tabula Rasa Press.

Tainter, Joe & Warren, G. L. 1971. *Salvage Excavations at the Fowler Site: Some Aspects of the Social Organization of the Northern Chumash, Skeletal Analysis of 4-SLO-406.* San Luis Obispo Archaeological Society Occasional papers No# 3&4.

Walsh, Jane M. 1976. *John Peabody Harrington, The Man and His California Indian Fieldnotes.* Ballena Press.

WPA eds. 1941. *Santa Barbara, A Guide to the Channel City and its Environs.* Hastings House.

Williamson, Ray A. 1984. *Living the Sky, The Cosmos of the American Indian.* Houghton Mifflin Company.

INDEX